My Secret Life

My Journey Through Domestic Violence

Mary Myles —

Thank you!

Lucy

#start by believing

Lisa Nicole Publishing
Lisanicolealexander.com
Gotha, FL 34734

Printed in the United States of America

Edits by Harley Dree and Rachel Schuetz

ISBN: 978-1-7356342-3-4

Table of Contents

Acknowledgement by Authors:

Tracy Rector: I dedicate my chapter to all survivors and child witnesses of domestic violence; may the sharing of my story help you find your voice and strength. I want to thank my husband, Greg, for being on this journey with me and showing me what true love is. I thank my adult children for being survivors along with me and being incredibly strong and loving adults. And to ALL the friends and family members who have been my support system through the difficult years after leaving, thank you. (And a special shout out to Chyna Robinson who said YES when I asked her to join me in making a film to raise awareness of DV.) Let's shine a light on domestic violence and raise awareness so one day we can end this toxic part of our culture.

Gabriella Smithers:

I dedicate my collaboration of this project to my mom, who always encouraged me as a child to write my thoughts and feelings down. I've carried these wise words close to my heart. I truly thank God for being the source of my strength and providing me with a circle of sisters that are like family. And lastly, to the victims who did not make it—may you all continue to Rest in Power. You will never be forgotten.

Theresa R. Simon: I want to thank my children Brianna, Bryce, and Brielle for being my reason why, and my strength. I am so blessed to be your mom. I want to thank my coach, Kenya Gray, for always encouraging me. To the survivors of domestic violence and narcissistic abuse, know that you are not alone, and you will be able to rebuild your life again.

Dr. Stacy L. Henderson-Shaw: Stacy LaTrelle Henderson, the innocent little girl who lost her voice as a child but now speaks from the heart and soul of the woman that I have become. Without your faith in God, I would not be alive today to tell our story. You are beautiful. You are strong. You are healed. You are loved. You are me. I am you. Together we are what God purposed us to be. We are VICTORIOUS! To our family, friends, loved ones, and everyone who we have met along our journey, "Thank You!" God Bless You! Love, Stacy

Donna Marie Lambert: I want to thank all of my coaches for helping me to fulfill one of my callings. To my children June, Dwayne Jr., & Julian for being the source of my strength to leave. To my mother for never judging me, S.I.P. and to my cousin Danielle "Chocolate " Govan who lost her life to Domestic Violence, S.I.P.

Madeliane Murphy: I want to thank the therapist's, alcohol and drug counselors, and family support workers for helping me. My children for journeying beside me and giving me the strength to carry on. My fabulous husband for breathing life back into me and never leaving me on my bad days. To everyone who reads this, please know you have the strength and courage: BELIEVE and NEVER give up.

Tonya K Austin: I want to take the time to dedicate this book to my children for loving and caring for me during my healing process. I also want to thank my ex-husband (Kiambu) for his last words spoken to me regarding my toxic situation; his voice reigned heavy during my transition from abused to survivor. Lastly, I want to thank God for allowing this wonderful opportunity to come falling directly in my lap! I love it, and I also want to thank myself---the emotional journey was hard, but I made it.

Introduction

This book is filled with stories of women that have survivied. They have survived different types of abuse from relationships where love was supposed to be what came from it. These pages are filled with sensitive issues of abuse and life altering occurances in each authors lives. Some names, locations, and identifying characteristics have been changed to protect the privacy of those depicted.

My hope is that as you read this book you are able to celebrate their bravery. My hope is that you will get this into the hands of someone that needs to know that what they are experiencing is not normal, and that it is abuse. My hope is that if you are reading it and are expereincing any of the things that you find throughout the pages that you will find the strength to call the number at the end of the book and reach out to resources that can help you. Know that you are not alone. You matter. You are loved. And you deserve to live a life that is free of abuse and filled with love.

Lisa Alexander M.S.
Founder & Executive Director
Stand Up Survivor
Lisa Nicole Publishing

Tracy Rector

Email: tracy.rector@gmail.com

Instagram: tracytrector

Facebook: Tracy Rector

Twitter: @TracyRector1

Film: *No Ordinary Love*, at NoOrdinaryLoveMovie.com

Facebook and Instagram: @noordinarylovemovie;

Twitter @NOLMovie

Tracy Rector, a survivor of domestic violence, helped to create an award-winning feature film, *No Ordinary Love*, (2019-20) to raise awareness of intimate partner violence. In her role as executive producer, she influenced the film to be authentic to the issue and to include spiritual abuse, reflective of her own experience. While serving on the board of directors for SafeHaven of Tarrant County (Texas; 2014-2020), she saw a tremendous need for greater awareness of domestic violence and sought to use film as the messenger. Her 23-year marriage to a minister fuels her passion to highlight spiritual abuse as an especially prevalent form of domestic violence in the south. She co-wrote an op-ed piece with the CEO of SafeHaven for the *Fort Worth Star-Telegram* in response to the president of a local seminary being forced to resign when his past statements reflecting his misogynistic theology came to light during the #MeToo movement.

She was interviewed about her personal story of an abusive marriage for an article in the FWST announcing her as the key-note speaker at a fundraising event for a domestic violence advocacy group that supports SafeHaven. She continues to shine a spotlight on intimate partner violence by sharing her personal story in great detail in this book to inspire other survivors to know there is hope for a fuller life away from their abuser. She lives with her loving and supportive husband of five years in Colleyville, Texas along with their newest addition, Lola, a Vizsla puppy.

A Glasshouse, an Elephant, and Eggshells

Valentine's Day, 2004. Flowers? Chocolates or a nice dinner out? My gift is a book. And I *love* books. But this book is *The Proper Care and Feeding of Husbands,* and it has sections highlighted to make sure I see them.

Wait. Let's back up several years. It's October 1982, we are just married, and before the wedding reception is over, I know this is going to be harder than I ever imagined. I spend a lot of our honeymoon alone because he needs to take a three-hour nap daily, and I'm not allowed in the room, and then the World Series is on, in Spanish, so. On day four when I tell the pool bartender that I'm on my honeymoon - after spending days by myself at the pool - he laughs and then later stops, aghast, when he sees us going to dinner together. In our first year of marriage, I cried more than all of the 22 previous years of my life combined. I'm not a crier. But he tells me in seminary he learned not to let women's tears manipulate him.

What have I done? Three months later, I'm pregnant. I'm beginning to realize that the "teasing" remarks he made about men and expected roles of women were closer to the truth in his mind. I'm working full time, he's a minister at a small church with time for a nap every day, and yet, each evening I cook dinner and clean up as he rests in his easy chair watching the news. I'm the new wife, so I acquiesce that this is the way it's going to be. I'm tired. As the months draw on, the pregnancy, work at work, work at home, begin to wear on me. I say something. But I'm told this is my role as the wife. God says so, it must be true.

The first few years are hard. I'm trying to adjust. I want this to work, but why is it so much work? The rules. There were many rules in this marriage, and any defiance was met with immediate rebuke. His food had to be cooked to specific standards, and if not met, he would spit it out in the trash. Soon I realize every infraction has a price. *You spend too much time with your family, you're my best friend now. You shouldn't want to go for a weekend away with your college roommate, I'm your best friend now.* I go anyway. So, I begin to measure if each time will be worth the cost of the emotional abuse later.

More rules. His shirts - after I iron them - must not be buttoned, at all. Sometimes I forget. I remember the first time. I walked into our closet and saw the four dress shirts I had carefully ironed in a heap on the floor, hangers broken in half. Seriously? This is what puts you into a rage? When I approach him about it, the gaslighting begins. I didn't know that term then, but the behavior is striking.

You did that on purpose. I told you not to button my shirts!
I'm not disrespectful, you are.
It's not my fault. You know I don't like that.
Really? Who has the anger problem? I'm not the one yelling.

It begins. I leave to get my haircut. When I come home, I'm met with scowls, silence. Like literal no-sound silence, walking-past-you-in-the-same-house silence and not-even-recognizing-you silence. I've never experienced anything remotely like this before. I ask what's wrong? Silence. Why are you mad? Silence. I'm confused. Then I'm hurt. And two... days... later...he approaches me with his Bible in hand. And he reads from Corinthians:

"It is disgraceful for a wife to cut off her hair....but if a woman has long hair, it is her glory."

So, there it is. My salvation is in jeopardy because I got a haircut? So, he says. Is this really what God thinks, what God wants of me? He says it's so, he's the minister, the man of God, the leader of the church, the "man of the household." Who am I? Do I even have a voice? Apparently, not so much.

Emotional and mental abuse is a gradual drip, drip, drip of shaming, ridicule, questioning, gaslighting and passive-aggressive behavior all to gain power and control over the victim. Even as a strong woman, I began to question everything I feel and think and do. He's the minister - and tells me regularly that he knows what God wants for me in my life. Each year I'm a little bit more broken with less and less of my self-worth available to push back against this constant abuse.

I knew early on in our marriage that something was wrong with the way we related to each other and thought we should go to counseling. When my suggestions for marriage counseling were not only ignored but ridiculed, I gave in and never pursued it until later, deciding simply to keep the peace. I desperately wanted to have a happy home for my children as they grew up. In hindsight, I wish I had insisted, although I'm not sure the outcome would have been different. He would always tell me that he does marriage counseling for a living and therefore he did *NOT* need someone else telling *him* how to do it. He was the expert.

I'm tough. I dig in. I can make it work. This is the life I chose. Besides, there's no way out. Divorce isn't an option. Baby number two is on the way. I love being a mom. I can do this.

Things are fine. Good, even. However, I do so much of THE THINGS. He works. He naps. Writes a sermon. He might take out the garbage. Then he sleeps. He gets up and works. Naps. Etc. Day in and day out. I'm so tired but I smile.

I go to church, two children in tow. The minister's wife. All eyes on us. We can't escape from the glasshouse. As the years go by, we move to other churches, but we're always living in the public eye. The secret. We have an abusive marriage living in a glasshouse with him, the elephant in the room. Everyone thinks we're the perfect family, and my contribution to the whole mess is I want them to think that, too. As the minister's family, our lives are in full view of the outside world, a.k.a. the congregation. In a glasshouse, smiles all around are expected, all the time.

I have these two precious children. I immerse myself in them. We have so much fun when the three of us are together. Then he comes home. Quiet. It's nap time. No, not the children, but his nap time. No one is allowed to talk, no TV, no music, no laughing. So, life stops. And then he wakes up, and we must smile. Because we're happy he is alive. Years later with my obedience to smile fading, he installs "happy bells" in the pantry to make sure I demonstrate my happiness. He insists we ring them when we're happy which should be a few times each day - right? He *needs* to know we are happy. I ask myself, what is this? It feels so controlling. He rings the bells. I refuse. But soon the children are ringing the bells to win his approval.

I long for another baby. I'm not sure why, but I convince myself that THIS time, he will help. He will be THE dad, THE husband to do the THINGS, to help, to be a partner in this thing called life. But alas, she cries in the night and he needs his precious sleep, so his foot in my back pushes me to go to her, to nurse her or comfort her, whatever she needs, even if it's just a soothing song or comforting rub. Something even a father could do. His shout of "God didn't give me the equipment" tells me he has no intention of ever disturbing his sleep, his comfort to go to her.

So, she and I are snuggling, with her at my breast; it's dark and Bob Tilton is on TV asking me to place my hand on the screen to receive God's blessing. God. Are you there? Is this for real? She's asleep now and I gently lay her down. It's morning. Repeat. Repeat. Sigh. Before I recognize it, this "elephant in the room" inside our glasshouse is growing.

Again, it's time for my haircut. Silence. More silence. I cannot stand it any longer, I finally apologize. Scripture reading. Sigh. Loneliness. *God, it's so lonely when you're on his side, and I'm over here by myself.* Life meanders on. The children are all in school and I continue to attempt to be the "perfect mother" and "perfect wife."

Children who have a mother who stays home with them are more intelligent, do better in school, and are happier in life. Don't you want this for our children?

Little did I know that his "nuggets of wisdom" were manipulation in disguise. So, I don't pursue a career but become the ultimate school-mom volunteer and look for part-time jobs that don't disrupt my main job of being wife and mother. I pour all my energy into creating a school-wide science fair, parent volunteer-led science labs, organize and run a creative problem-solving program for 100 children at the school all which serve as a distraction to the reality of our messy glasshouse. One of the dads at the school thanked me for my volunteering efforts and said I could be the CEO of a big corporation - to this day I consider this one of the best compliments I've ever received.

I thought about his kind words. My husband never recognized my contributions, always unwilling to help. He couldn't understand why I was spending so much time doing things for other peoples' children. That our children should be my first (and obviously only) priority. Then I realized what he was trying to say. *He* should be my first priority. When I was busy contributing to others, he complained when dinner wasn't sufficient or if I wasn't keeping up with my household chores. It became clear that my primary focus was to be sure his comfort was never compromised.

Throughout our marriage, he would admonish me when I did not meet his needs, or if I disappointed him, or disagreed with him. I always walked on eggshells trying not to upset the elephant in the room. Sometimes his punishment would be silence. He would act as if I did not exist at all. Just like after a haircut, he walked right past me in the house and would not look at me, speak to me or acknowledge I was present. This would go on for hours and sometimes a couple of days – depending on how long I could last. Other times when I rebuked his attempts at power and control, he would bring his Bible and read from Ephesians:

"Wives be subject to your husbands as you are to the Lord. For the husband is the head of the wife just as Christ is the head of the church...Just as the church is subject to Christ, so also wives ought to be, in   everything, to their husbands."

But he stopped reading before the next verse:

"Husbands, love your wives, just as Christ loved the church."

As this behavior continued, my heart began to close - without me noticing at first. I grew numb. I tried to stay focused on being a mom, creating a fun space within our glasshouse so my children could experience a happy home. At least that's what I thought.

The spiritual abuse was the hardest. His gross, misogynistic view of scripture and theology drove his need to even have power and control over my relationship with God and the church. I questioned a lot of my 'beliefs' as they did not sit well with my strong, female core. I still don't call what I am experiencing abuse. My thoughts are of emotional exhaustion, disrespect and loneliness. We didn't talk about emotional abuse in the '80's and '90's. Honestly, I thought domestic violence was violent. I didn't know it was mostly about power and control. Any talk of domestic abuse at that time included references to the films *The Burning Bed* and *Sleeping with the Enemy* which depicted egregious examples of the worst kind of intimate partner violence. Thirty and 40 years ago, this sort of thing was still considered a "private matter." The first domestic violence shelters didn't begin to appear in the US until the mid to late '70's.

He never lost an opportunity to ridicule what is important to me: my high school, college alma mater, musicians I like, organizations I joined - nothing was off limits. I joined the Junior League in our town. When I had an evening activity, the emotional price was pretty high. I had to make sure I gave him plenty of notice if he needed to babysit his own children. He questioned why I needed to 'buy' my friends likening it to being in my sorority in college. While setting up for the big fundraising event with all the new members, I watched the other husbands happily helping with whatever needed to be done. I may not have been, but I felt like the only one without a supportive husband there. The reality was crushing. Before the end of my first year in the league, I decided it wasn't worth the emotional cost. I resigned soon after.

One of my part-time jobs was to write the newsletter for the domestic violence shelter in our town. I enjoyed the challenge of the research, writing and designing the small publication. Once while researching for an interview, I came across a list of 10 characteristics of an abusive marriage. My jaw dropped. My heart pounded in my chest. Stunned, my marriage fit at least seven of the 10. But I couldn't have an abusive marriage. He never hit me, I never had bruises, never went to the emergency room. There was a deadline.

Dinner to be made, homework, baths and no time to give this another thought. I buried it. I wasn't ready to face the consequences of embracing this truth.

Before I knew it, we're going to my 20th high school reunion. How can this be? Everyone was asked to submit a small paragraph with an update on our lives, family, work and adventures to be compiled in a class booklet. I wrote a paragraph worthy of being envied by all with our perfect little family going on all our exotic adventures to Europe living our best life. Wait, what? What was I thinking? Looking back, I'm surprised at my lack of awareness to the disconnect between my reality and what I wanted everyone to see. My secret life. That sounds so exotic. Secret life. But how else do you live, but in secret, in a glasshouse walking on eggshells with an elephant in every room taking up so much space no one else can breathe? As a victim of mental and emotional abuse, you begin to live in two different realities. The one you want everyone to see and know shoved up next to the daily barrage of 'you're never going to be good enough.' Shame and failure come crashing into your inner core. The life you imagined with a happy marriage and a family is so very far from what you are living every.... single.... day. The next high school reunion would prove to be quite different.

Throughout our marriage, any problems we had were basically because of me - according to him - and my lack of _____ (fill in the blank). He often ridiculed my college alma mater, saying it was mediocre academics, since it was in West Texas. So, of course, I didn't know things. He has three degrees. He was far more knowledgeable and experienced in understanding relationships and marriage, and, well, just about everything. He's a minister. A counselor. He was the minister-counselor-teacher and would 'help me understand' what we needed to do to make our relationship better. Early in the marriage, I accepted this partly due to our age difference and his higher degree of education, and largely due to my naiveté. As the years pass, I grow less and less tolerant at his "corrections." He never respected my ability to know how to do something or handle any situation. I had to yield to his way a disproportionate amount of the time.

I now know that many abusive relationships include financial abuse. Abusers use money and finances to manipulate and maintain power and control over their victim. This creates dependence and requires obedience and constant compliance. Again, I did not realize it at the time, but his idea of giving *me* complete control over our finances was abusive in his own passive-aggressive way. He would declare that is not he a kind and wonderful husband because he gives up control over the finances and allows me to be in charge of all of it. Paying bills, banking, investments, taxes, setting up anything new that requires a payment, refinancing loans - literally everything. He had no interest in dealing with any of these tasks or decisions. I am supposed to be grateful that he allows me to have all the "power."

One day, I am sitting at my desk near the back door to the garage, knee deep in preparing the paperwork to send to our accountant as Tax Day nears. Ministers had certain tax breaks for housing expenses (at lease they did at that time) which required a lot of record keeping and compiling at year's end. I am not a finance person. This is not my favorite activity. Not even close. I have piles of statements and stacks of receipts (this is back when everything was printed) with a calculator humming. The garage door goes up, but I barely register the sound. It's only 11 a.m. He's home early for lunch. On most days, he would go to the church for a few hours and return home for lunch. After his usual afternoon nap, he would return to the church for a couple hours and be home well before dinner. He required enormous amounts of attention when he was home. The few hours he was away is when I got THINGS done.

He walks through the door, and without looking at him, I say hello and keep focused on my work at hand. I can sense that he is just standing there, looking at me. I sigh and say I'm really busy and can't talk right now. He is still there. He demands that I stand up. He wants to show me something. I plead to have another 20 minutes - to no avail. Like I said before, enormous amounts of attention. So, I get up. He wants to show me the proper way to greet your husband when he walks through the door after working to support the family. I am livid. *You have got to be kidding. You have only been gone for a couple hours!* He reaches for me and pulls me into a hug. I push away and get back to the taxes. The pouting ensues. I don't remember it, but I'm fairly certain the silencing began as well. It's funny, after years of that bothering me, I grew to welcome it. He would leave me alone.

The stress of being in this non-partnership marriage was beginning to take its toll. In our glasshouse, if Dad was not happy, life was miserable. Even on the toughest days, and they weren't all hard, I didn't think about leaving the marriage. I never saw that as an option.

As a woman of faith, I took my vow of 'til death do us part' seriously. The honest truth was - I didn't take a vow of misery and being in a marriage with emotional, verbal, spiritual and somewhat physical abuse is miserable. But I still did not see my marriage as "abusive," I just knew it was hard. I thought I was supposed to stick it out, to stay together for the children, and more importantly that's what God wanted me to do. When he spoke about marriage from the pulpit or in conversation, divorce was not an option. With what seemed like a personal message to me, he made sure to say studies show children of divorce do poorly in school, grow up to have unsuccessful lives, etc., etc. As our children began to approach the teenage years, I began to see that being in a dysfunctional marriage can also have detrimental effects on children. Is this what I want my daughters to see as acceptable behavior from their future partners or husbands? I was not modeling the marriage I hoped for them to have.

Victims face the conundrum of is it harder to stay or harder to leave? For a while, it just seems easier to live with the devil you know than the one of uncertainty. As the elephant in our glasshouse grew larger than life, whatever love was there at one time dissipated and the void began to fill with emotional detachment.

Then, my father died unexpectedly. My dad, the healthier-than-most 65-year-old, dropped dead while jogging. You can't describe the chaos around you when you lose a loved one without warning. I remember walking out of the hospital emergency room to go to my car and seeing the traffic lights turn from red to green, traffic flowing as normal. I wanted to shout, STOP! How can you carry on as if all systems are normal? The shock lingers as you have to go through the motions of what comes next. My mom and dad together - their marriage - was my go-to for stability. He was gone in an instant, and it felt like my whole world caved in. I knew my life was hard, my marriage difficult, but until now, I could deal with it. All these years I struggled to hold this crumbling, cold, stone statue-of-a-marriage together. My husband's continual abuse created fractures in the glasshouse that my smile could no longer hide.

I was so deeply sad and grieving but he says I'm stuck in the grieving process and need to snap out of it. He's a minister and knows these things, he says, he deals with it regularly. I hardly care to know the answer but ask anyway, please explain. Two months have passed, and dinner meals were substandard, too many nights with leftovers, and the laundry hadn't been done in several weeks, clearly signs to him that I had a problem with grief. As I continue to grieve, I begin to disappear inside myself. I pull away from him emotionally because I cannot bear the pain of it while my heart is broken. It's almost a full year before I begin to attempt to figure out how to navigate my life again. I have to, my first-born is heading off to college. There are THINGS to do.

I go through the motions for a while. Then, as I always do, I pull myself out of the hole and go on, doing what I can to create a happy home for us. After almost a year of grieving, I'm unwilling to continue with the same routines we had fallen into. And although I couldn't name it yet, I was tiring of the emotional abuse. I cannot live the rest of my life carrying the vast majority of the load of having a family. It was more than just about the THINGS. He needs to step up, participate, be an active part of this family. Plus, I was exhausted from never being able to live up to the ever-increasing expectations of being a good wife and mother.

I was not willing to continue carrying all the pieces by myself. I wanted to renegotiate our arrangement in how our relationship worked. I asked him to be more involved in the family affairs, the work involved in running a household and family. He was not interested in having his perfect world disrupted. I knew that I was not 'allowed' to give him a honey-do list. The one time I gave him a list, he rumpled it up in my face and threw it in the trash announcing he did not do lists. I could ask him to do one thing at a time and when he got around to doing it, then, and only then, could I ask him to do something else. He had total veto power – if he didn't want to do something, he simply wouldn't do it. It was way past time to change the way we did things.

I wrote down a list of about 75% of all the THINGS that I did on a regular basis to run the house and family. It was a long list with a variety of tasks. I asked him to choose some of the things on the list that he was willing to take over, to share some of the burden I carried mostly alone; I did not tell him which ones to do, I gave him the choice. I knew any other way would be met with instant resistance, and I wanted this to improve our marriage.

In his typical passive-aggressive way, he chose to do something that wasn't even on the list – to do his own laundry – his laundry, not anyone else's. This didn't even help at all since, at the time, I would still be doing laundry for three people. To try to ease into this new routine, I agreed to his terms. This was disappointing enough, but every time we were out socializing with others, I got to hear him announce to everyone how domesticated he is because he did his own laundry. He would chat with the women and 'share' stain removal tips. Then I would hear what a blessing my wonderful husband is because he does the laundry. Upon hearing this, he shot a sarcastic grin my direction revealing his subliminal message about my list of THINGS. The elephant grew a little bigger. I let the resentment build without addressing it head on. My heart continued to drift away from this so-called marriage as I felt more and more disrespected.

He always had the notion that, because we were married, my body was his and he could do with it what he wanted – whenever he felt like it. His version of physical abuse never left bruises on the outside, but little by little it destroyed me on the inside. He viewed my body as his property. He would come up to me - face to face - and grope one of my breasts. We were never in a romantic setting when this happened. Most of the time, I was standing in the kitchen preparing a meal. As he was facing me, he would grope my breast so hard he would push me backwards. To prevent me from falling backwards, he would place his free hand behind my shoulder and hold me steady while his other hand gripped my breast. I ALWAYS objected to his advances like this. I begged him to stop. I tried to explain that this was quite uncomfortable, even painful, and certainly was not romantic. He would say, "It's ok, we're married" and "don't be so cold." I began pulling up one knee and crossing my arms over my chest to block him when I realized he was about to do this. After my rejection, sometimes he would bring his Bible and read from Matthew's gospel:

"a man shall leave his father and mother and be joined to his wife, and the two shall become one flesh. So, they are no longer two but one flesh."

He began to sense my pulling away, my emotional detachment growing, so his emotional and physical neediness increased exponentially. The more my heart closed in, the more he demanded to be verbally reassured of my love and devotion. My tepid response was met with more neediness and passive-aggressive behavior, which looks like this. He never mastered the grill mainly because he didn't want to. So, I was the grill chef in addition to being responsible for all the other cooking. One evening I was rushing from the outdoor grill to the kitchen back and forth to have everything done around the same time. He was, of course, relaxing on the couch watching TV. As I rush past him, he grabs my arm and asks why don't I stop on my way back and forth and rub his shoulders or scratch his back?

I know. Right? Seriously? As I wiggle out of his grasp, I assure him that won't be happening, but he could sure get up and help with dinner. As I walk back to the kitchen, I stomp on the eggshells not caring as they metaphorically break under my feet. He scowls. Sighs. Pouts. I've long been used to ignoring the behavior, but it weighs on me. Heavy.

It is early 2004. We have a junior in college, a senior in high school and a middle schooler. As we all know, having a high school senior creates a lot of moving parts with meetings and appointments along with college preparations to juggle. I was co-chair of the Project Graduation, which proved to be a great distraction to what had become my daily status of misery.

Then, it's Valentine's Day. Yes, THAT Valentine's Day with the book. We never made much of this holiday, so my expectations were pretty low especially considering the current climate of our relationship. Looking back, I can't imagine what he was thinking. Our marriage is in shambles, an emotional desert. My smiles are all but faded away. No reason to ring the bells in the pantry even if I would. The glasshouse is as open as ever, but I have less energy to hide the truth. My gift, the book - *The Proper Care and Feeding of Husbands* - is met with my immediate disdain. It's the Phyllis Schlafly version of being the perfect housewife supporting her man. I refuse to even open it. He keeps giving it back to me explaining that numerous women have thanked him for suggesting this book to them, how it has saved their marriage. I sigh, exhausted from the conversation. He begs me to at least open it. When I do, I see several pages have yellow highlighter on key sections. So, he read the book and left his yellow highlighter on places where I am supposed to give careful attention. I remember thinking it was as if he "peed" his yellowness on the areas that explain where I need to improve as a wife. The book falls to the floor and I walk away. It reappears at my

bathroom sink the next morning. We play this game for a few days

until it disappears for good. What lingers is a despondent emptiness

and overwhelming sense of my life...will.... never.... change. I will

never be good enough in his eyes, never measure up, never give

enough, never do enough, never be enough. I feel like I'm falling,

and I don't even care if or where I land.

    We are headed to see our son for parents' weekend. In the

parking lot at the airport, he reaches in the trunk to get his sport coat,

still on the hanger from the cleaners. He quickly tries to put it on as

the shuttle is pulling up. It's buttoned. He struggles and then throws

it down, furious. How could I do this to him *today, of all days*? How

many times do I have to be told not to button his shirts and jackets?

The silence, again. I've ruined his day when it was supposed to be

such a happy one to see and celebrate our college student. This time,

with my resolve still in low supply, I get angry, no, not really angry, I

cease to care. I approach the gate agent and ask to be moved to

another seat. It's a full flight, my lucky day. We fly in silence. Once

we arrive, I manage to find my smile and pull it out of its hiding place.

I don't know if our son can sense the tension, but I do my best to

mask it with smiles and hugs.

    I struggled every day with how our marriage had deteriorated.

I could feel myself sinking into a hole. He tells me that I should just

be happy - I have "everything any woman could ever wish for - a

husband who loves me, three great kids, a nice home," etc. In his

often-used minister/counselor I-know-better-than-you tone, he told me I should do something for others, volunteer somewhere, because that would make me happy. He also suggested I should pray more. And the kicker - if I would just give my whole heart to him - like I had before - everything would be perfect again – the way it used to be. In other words, the reason our marriage is a mess is because of me, something I've done or haven't done, and if I would just listen to him, everything would be wonderful like it used to be.

He was in panic power-and-control mode. He told me my salvation was in jeopardy because I was rejecting God's will for my life. I was breaking my vow to him before God. How could I do this to our children? Each morning he placed a prayer card by my bathroom sink, that in this context, was a horrific prayer:

Saint Michael the Archangel, defend us in battle. Be our protection against the wickedness and snares of the devil; May God rebuke him, we humbly pray; And do thou, O Prince of the Heavenly Host, by the power of God, thrust into hell Satan and all evil spirits who wander through the world for the ruin of souls. Amen

Without realizing it was happening, I gradually became depressed with what I learned later in therapy was situational anxiety depression. After once again unsuccessfully begging him to go to therapy with me to work on our marriage, a year after *the book*, I began going to counseling alone. I desperately needed to find out why my marriage was so difficult, why I was emotionally and physically exhausted almost all the time and so miserable. My husband ridiculed me and made fun of the books I was reading as suggested by the psychologist. After a month of weekly therapy, my counselor read a list of characteristics. He wanted to know my reaction. My tears gave away my emotions. The list described my husband to a T. My therapist shared his suspicions with me that he felt there was a strong possibility that his behaviors were consistent with a personality disorder. I was stunned. *You mean to tell me that there are other people like him in this world?* I quickly learned there is nothing, and I mean nothing, I could do to change him, to fix his psychological disorder-- but I tried. With help from my therapist, I gave him five more months to prove he could turn this sinking ship around.

About four weeks before we separated (when he knew our marriage was in serious trouble), I came home after working a long day, with grocery sacks in my hands, and he greeted me in the garage with this. "I'm going to show you how you greet someone that you love when they come home. First you get a kiss, and a hug (he kisses and hugs me) and then you get a squeeze," and he proceeded to squeeze both my breasts as I stood there with both hands full. I slung the full bags at him and yelled, *"Don't you ever do that to me again,"* and vowed to myself that would be the last time he ever touched me.

I knew my life was hard, my marriage was difficult, but I come from strong mid-western stock, which means I'm tough, and I'm no quitter. Plus, my faith and my church said I must stick it out - you know that whole 'til death do us part' thing. After over 20 years of marriage, I finally reached my breaking point. I knew I had to climb out of the darkness, push to the surface that female strength in my DNA and leave my abuser. I finally realized and accepted the fact that I was never going to be good enough or smart enough, and, most assuredly, I couldn't do this for the rest of my life. Plus, I knew I needed to do something to show my children I didn't see our marriage as a good example for them of a healthy relationship.

I want a divorce. I finally said the words that were lingering in the air for months.

Our glasshouse was cracking even more. We were all still miserable - because the elephant was miserable - for two long, painful weeks until I finally insisted, he had to move out. He did, but under great protest. Sixty days later, he was served divorce papers. The separation lasted a long 18 months. He used every delay tactic possible, even requesting a jury trial, which is rare in family court creating an even longer delay.

Once we separated, he began to stalk me, cruising up and down the street. He called and sent emails numerous times saying I would ruin our children's lives, no one would ever want me as an old divorcée. I got long 3 - 4-page letters typed and printed on paper with red roses on the borders pleading with me to come to my senses, to do it for the children.

I would come home to find packages from him inside the house letting me know he had been there. I consistently asked him to stop. One day I came home to find him lingering outside the house, and he followed me in - letting me know that in the eyes of God we were still married suggesting what that meant to him. With my heart pounding, fearing the worst, I quickly walked toward the back door, got in my car and fled. First, I called my lawyer to begin proceedings to obtain a restraining order and then a locksmith. I handed my lawyer a huge box of everything he sent to me including books on marriage and a copy of the Kirk Cameron film *Fireproof.* The restraining order came quickly and proved to be a godsend as it kept him away. The fear he instilled in me during the stalking still haunts me to this day. I cannot go to bed each night without physically seeing that every door is locked.

Throughout the separation, we continued to live in a glasshouse as our personal business seemed to be everyone's business. The phone would ring. A parishioner wanted to give advice of how to repair our marriage. A 'friend' would call to try to talk me out of the divorce, apparently knowing this was not what Jesus wanted for me. He was asking people to contact me since he couldn't. A parishioner called to apologize for the church taking so much of his time as pastor causing stress on our marriage. The rumors were flying because I wasn't saying a word. Someone called to congratulate me on my upcoming marriage. I asked her who I was marrying, because that sounded pretty exotic and I could use some exotic about now. I received letters from people, lots of letters and cards all with the same message - *how could you do this, divorce is evil, you're a terrible mother for doing this to your children, he's a wonderful, holy man who doesn't deserve this.* Friends fell away. My life was too complicated. He was their minister, what did I expect them to do?

As I reflect on our marriage, I see how I could have dealt with our conflicts differently, which may have prevented some of my resentment that built up over the years. Gradually, slowly, my normal became something that was completely unacceptable. Why did I stay? I've often been asked and even asked myself that question. I desperately wanted a happy home for our children to grow up in, and any conflict between him and me was an emotionally painful process for me. It just became easier to go along than to put up a struggle. My self-worth was diminished to the point of being unrecognizable. I was living in a glasshouse with an elephant in the room while walking on eggshells in a mine field. Whew, no wonder I was exhausted all the time.

I look at where I am now, and I don't even know the person I was before. The abuse made me a different person. It's been over a decade since I became legally free from my abusive husband. I still get tears in my eyes just thinking about what I put my children and my extended family through trying to make it work. It took me years to realize I was in an abusive marriage. I was fortunate enough to not ever need to go to an emergency shelter. I never had bruises. Never had a reason to go to the ER, but the abuse gradually destroyed my self-worth and nearly broke my spirit.

Is there a happy ending? Yes, indeed. I was convinced I would never marry again. Well, as they say, never say never. A few years later, I met an amazing man who is kind, smart, loving, respectful, supportive, and full of life and laughter. Our blended family is the perfect combination of healthy love that we all so desperately needed.

I served for seven years on the board of directors for our local domestic violence agency, SafeHaven of Tarrant County (Texas), which became part of my healing process. From that experience, I realized there is a tremendous need for raising awareness of intimate partner violence. So, I produced a film to help raise awareness. *No Ordinary Love* is an award-winning feature film showing in film festivals, but hopefully soon to be available for streaming to raise awareness of domestic violence in every home across the US. If you are currently in an abusive relationship, please reach out to your local domestic violence agency, call the national hotline, tell someone, and create a safety plan to leave. You are worthy and can break free.

The author's daughter, Alban Rector, wrote the poem *Breaking Free* as a child witness of domestic violence.

Let us not forget the emotional effect on the children who witness domestic violence.

Breaking Free

She was young and green,
Like the first flower of spring.
Beautiful, inside and out.
Precious without a doubt.

Her opportunities were endless.
Destined for success.
Hope for the future
She was sure he loved her.

He asked and she said yes.
She never would have guessed
what the next 20 years would hold,
or that his heart could be so cold.

She'd keep her promise somehow.
But once she took that vow
His true colors were revealed
Her pain she must conceal.

Forced to upkeep the perfect image,
Almost like being in a cage.

Her love wilted. Her hope snuffed out.
For a long time, she lived without
All that she deserved.
To think, he had the nerve.

Always had to be right.
Demanding the spotlight.
Expecting the world, giving nothing in return.
She began to yearn.

For something. Something more.
Couldn't keep her fenced in anymore.
Took some time to figure out
She could run. So look out.

Now nothing stands between her and freedom.
The past she has overcome.
She's wild and free,
Just as it should be.

Sailing on the open sea.

Gabriella Smithers

Gabriella Smithers has been a native of Richmond, Va. for over thirty years where she was adopted by the Smithers and the Jackson family as a baby and readopted as an adult by the Short family. She is an honors graduate of Varina High School; obtained her Associates degree in Criminal Justice Administration- Magna Cum Laude and her bachelor's degree in criminal justice - Cum Laude from Strayer University. Despite the circumstances of her tumultuous marriage, she has remained steadfast in the foundation of her Christian faith taught to her as a child, to provide her strength and comfort.

God blessed her with three wonderful sons, Isaac, Samuel and Nathanael, who are the driving force for her to press forward in the goals she had long forgotten.

Her passion is about "Women who are ready to win their hearts back". She is a community activist and recycling advocate. Gabriella loves her church, singing and especially baking. She dedicates this penned story to the memory her mother, Aeyrer Lannaese Jackson-Smithers and grandmother, Virginia Belle Smithers-Edwards.

Missing Person's Report: A Marriage Story of a Lost Soul
My Story with reflective poetic excerpts

I am Jamaican American! I didn't know that until 2001 but you'll find out about that later. This story is about the love of my life. He was a handsome, green eyed Italian American. His intelligence was inspiring, and he captivated me by our conversations. He was so full of wisdom and brought a sense of laughter that I had lost along the way. When we met, I was at the end of a high school not so fairy tale relationship and wound up being hurt. He swooned me just by being a listening ear, providing all this advice about love and life... and how he would treat me if we dated. I was falling hard but afraid to get back into a relationship. I was told all the right things to encourage me to go against my better judgement. I could not understand why my friends constantly questioned me about him.

I began to distance myself because I thought there was a jealousy factor that was in play. Eventually, I lost some of those friends because they could see things that I could not, and I was unwilling to take heed. Ironically, the loudest voice was my roommate who was so upset with my decision to marry him that she refused to be a bridesmaid after being asked. Her last words to me were, "You'll end up dead with the likes of him!" I was full of emotions, but angry and hurt topped them. While we still shared a room, we never spoke again. I wish I could apologize to those friends now, especially her. Regret and shame of my naïve and immature decisions have had life-long consequences.

I wish I had known that love didn't hurt in 2002. As a 17-year-old college student, what did I truly know about the work it would take to have a God-fearing relationship and stable marriage? He had already started exposing explosive antics early on. Before I pledged, vowed my life and gave my soul to a man who already didn't value me as I did in him, I should have not allowed myself to be swept up in the mantra of "I will love him so much that my love will force him to love me, appreciate me, adore me, cherish me and then he will make positive changes to how he approaches me."

I wish I had known that my lack of self-love would obliterate my existence, or his lack of love would encourage me to isolate myself. After so many years of isolation, my detachment is now a comfort. Even now, years after my divorce has been finalized, I still have to fight myself on not sequestering my feelings as well as also from hiding from people. Daily, I say out loud to myself- "Shine today! You get nowhere degrading yourself!"

SELF DEGRADATION

I gave of myself and you helped tear me down,

ripping me to pieces and enjoying the flames that ignited.

Burning the remnants of life that resided within me,

my soul dark with resentment, bitterness and hurt.

My eyes forever damp from the tears that escapes my lids,

neck tense from withholding the pressures within.

Body shaking, wrecked with the emotion welled inside, trying to push

out,

Trying to push out through the pores of my being, only I won't allow

it.

Fear of seeing it, feeling, it, going through it,

my inner mind can't take the weight of the world involving this love,

I can't breathe, chest heavy, lungs gasping for air.

It's a beautifully sad reminder that that kind of "love" never changes,

heartaches come in the mornings.

Where sunrises, a beautiful entity, should bring forth renewal and

refreshment,

reminders of the past lingered and the hurt from my yesterday's rise

again.

It might help to know how I got to a place where I accepted the abuse as normal and stayed for almost a decade. One of the myths that domestic abuse statistics state is that a percentage of victims of domestic violence grew up in a home [or environment] where one viewed it, heard it, or lived it. This couldn't be furthest from the truth in my story. I grew up in a close-knit family, deeply rooted in the Christian faith, full of love, family dinners and trips, game nights and full-fledged singing, belting out tunes type of home.

How could "I" fall victim to a man who was completely the opposite of who my daddy was? I consider daddy to be a gentle giant, and I was a daddy's girl through and through. We would play baseball and he would hone in on developing my track techniques-pruning me to be track star. I never was, but in my daddy's eyes you could not tell him anything different since I would beat my own personal goals. My mom believed in encouraging a strong set of moral character traits and motivated me to strive for the very best academically. They supported all my endeavors from creating a school recycling club I started in middle school, to various community service organizations, band, track, volleyball, you name it!

One fate filled spring day, I learned I was not who I thought I was. I learned I truly did not belong. I was adopted. All this time, I thought I was biologically my parent's child. I mean, I was dark brown, my daddy was dark brown. Even though my cousins always teased me and told me I was adopted, I never believed them. My world spiraled out of control and everything to me had been a life of deceit. I felt unloved by my parents and my biological parents, lied to by my entire family [even though it wasn't their place to tell me the truth], and completely unwanted and abandoned by my biological parents. The friends I disclosed this information to did not see this news as a big deal. After trying to reason with them, to no avail on my standpoint I finally realized that they wouldn't get it- they had biological connections to their parents, they wouldn't and couldn't possibly understand me and my hurts.

I left for college that same summer, unhealed, wounded, broken, and determined to find a new family. Perfect prey for a predator! Being an only child- naturally, I was a loner. His pick-up line: "Stop sitting by yourself, come sit next to me," flashing his beautiful set of perfect white teeth and his green eyes twinkled. [We shared a biology lab course together.] I felt honored that such a handsome man even looked at me, let alone spoke to me. I moved from my lab table to his and breathed in his cologne. He smelled of the outdoors with hints of sandalwood. Similar to the scent my daddy wore.

I took this small similarity as a great form of kismet. I knew I couldn't stay angry at my parents forever, and these little reminders made my anger at them subside. I began to call them and chat, however, never mentioning I was seeing someone. We began dating shortly after and he continued to make me swoon, wined and dined me. We studied together and took walks on the beach or around campus. Me talking and him giving advice. I fell head over heels in love. There were moments throughout this time where I noticed he would clinch his fists. He would glare at me or he would get upset with me about things I did not understand. I did not know what warranted that level of negative emotion, but I brushed them all off because I was determined to be everything he needed so that we could be together. When he asked me to marry him after a few months of dating, I felt this was God's calling for me. I had gone away to school praying for another family- here it was, this gift, or so I thought. I accepted the proposal, but my only condition was that we find a church to begin attending together. I was still deeply rooted in my faith and I knew from my upbringing that mama and daddy would accept him if he was a person that valued God.

I embellished a great deal to my parents on who he was so that I could force the marriage to proceed forward. I so terribly wanted something of my own. While my parents and I were on speaking terms, I was still hurt about the first seventeen years of my life and the lie that rested there. My efforts and lies about who I portrayed him to be sufficed for them and we married that winter. Nine months later [the first six of those months he was away in military basic training], he backhanded me at the dinner table because I questioned him on a topic we were discussing. I was more in shock than anything and I conjured up several reasons as to why I was to blame for my swelling jaw.

I promised myself to never talk back or question his authority again. What used to be a charismatic, extroverted butterfly became a docile, introverted caterpillar. I secluded myself in my self-made cocoon, only going out to attend church, visit the commissary or the library and return home. I begin taking online college courses, since I chose to drop out years earlier and support the marriage wherever his life took us. He said he supported my continuing secondary education as long as I held down the responsibilities he required for the house. That was sometimes hard to manage contingent on my educational workload.

I wish I had known that no amount of makeup could cover the scars, the open internal wounds. My foundation perfectly hid my black eyes, bite marks, welts on my cheeks or handprints on my neck but my whole heart was damaged and completely broken. Torn in half. Lifeless. My plastered smile was worn, and my eyes lacked the vibrancy they once held. That first time it happened, my "I'm sorry" reward was a bracelet, flowers, and my favorite meal. Why didn't I walk away then? No children were involved at this time. Nevertheless, I had this innate desire to change him, that I could help him.

Would a baby help him love me? I became pregnant but the violence and the severity of that violence would increase. I was confused at what was happening. In my immature and young mind, I thought giving him a baby would bring us both happiness. Yet, I was the only one full of joy. I finally had someone of my own that would love me in return. The pregnancy was turbulent. I would endure being pushed, shoved, kicked, punched, thrown into dressers, head bashed against oven vent hoods, spit on, bit, cursed and yelled at, and then given the silent treatment.

When I developed the nerve to tell someone at church [several years into the marriage], I was told to stop lying. The image he portrayed at church was totally against who I was telling them he was behind closed doors. I completely shut down and dedicated my life to ensuring the unborn baby lived. I desperately wanted to love someone, and they reciprocate it. Our baby son entered this world and I melted in love. His little life gave me the will to live, but not enough for me to leave. I was petrified to make that type of bold move. I hoped that I could bear the suffering from my then husband so that my son could have a two-parent household like I did. Not all two-parent households are healthy as such was this case. I became pregnant again and lost all my will to fight. I had had another son as we got the news that we were being relocated to another Air Base and he would have to complete a deployment tour before we could get stationed at the new base.

Deployments were glorious to me. I could breathe. I enjoyed those moments of solitude where I would inhale and exhale and fear was not in the equation. I had the most fun with my sons, baking together and making an utter mess, playing in the yard and leaving the toys out for the next day's play time, sleeping soundly with my sons on each side of me. It was pure bliss.

I never slept the night before he was due to return, my nerves would be completely frazzled. I spent the week prior cleaning profusely and making meals. Everything had to be perfect. I always wanted to make a good impression. The welcome home was consistently sweet, and I always thought that he had changed, but the peace and the sweetness never lasted.

There were many instances were various family members would get glimpses of me or would hear a rumor and attempt to connect with me, but I was terrified that if I went along and the plan failed, the repercussions would be detrimental. It seemed easier to just keep quiet and pretend that the world I was living in was safe, therefore making the world believe that I was okay. I lost many family members who couldn't continue a relationship with me due to feeling that my potential death would be on their conscience. In my years of growth, I see that this was a move out of maintaining a sense of personal sanity and self-health for themselves.

*Untitled [written a few days after returning home after running with my children to safety]

Mind whirling
In overload
Overthinking
I'm going to fold

Directionless
Pointless
End game unknown
Forward backward
Standstill

Which way
Due north
Move forth

Tears fall from my heart
Instead of my eyes

Burning flames encase the moat of my soul
Smoke squeezing the breath of life from me
Blinded by the tunnel my irises see
Limbs stilted like a marionette

My senses controlled by your actions
Thoughts ruining my peace
Unsettled climate within

Forecasted predictions- tsunami
Chance of winds reaching deadly force
drawbridge needs cover

The castle in danger, destruction near
Synapses pinging
Everything ringing
Inner me crying
Something is dying
Flowers blooming
Petals fuming
Need water, quench my thirst
Will I ever be first
Has the rain come
Where are you from

Leave me in despair
Feigning for air

Lungs collapsing
Gasping
Last breath
I've left

Floating between the embers and vapors

Throw me in the fire, ball me up like paper
This cycle spinning my body
Empty, weightless, ashes Gone...

Rebirth is glistening. HE is sustaining
No longer maintaining,
Reviving

By 2014, I was dead on the inside. Willing him to just "do it" and get it over with, my piercing eyes locked in on his as he strangled me. I was looking down at him as he held me by my neck above him. I did not kick or try to writhe my way from his grasp. My eyes said it all and he lost all enjoyment to continue his plight as he tossed me aside in disgust. At 0300 on December 8, 2014, I finally called someone to rescue me- my dad. I told him I needed to come home. He made the six-hour journey down to my house in South Carolina and we packed my truck, his truck, my children and headed back "home"- Richmond, Va. I have never looked back!!

He served me with divorce papers on January 4, 2015. I signed and returned them happily! I cut all my hair off on February 14, 2015. I made a new vow to myself as I shredded all of the hurts, pains, loneliness, and defeat with each strand of hair that fell to the barber shop floor. Tears flowed down my cheeks but this time it was tears of freedom.

My Vow

This Proclamation is issued by Gabriella Smithers-Twine containing among other things my status as an adult woman. To wit that on this day, all pieces of my mind, heart and spirit held in slavery to the unrealistic, overwhelming, and overbearing expectations and limitations of this imagined marriage shall be thenceforward and forever free. The party present will recognize and maintain this freedom. And will do no acts of repressed such liberty and that I can reclaim my voice, identity, & authority of all areas of my life that pertain to me. Vow excerpt written by Iyanla Vanzant

It's now 2020, and what a journey of restoration, rebuilding and renewing I've been on. I returned back to college and received two degrees. I purchased a home with a big yard for my boys after taking two years to save a proper down payment. I've established a career in law enforcement which I love and get to encounter people where my experience is crucial in detection. And I'm passionate about sharing my story to save other individuals and children.

Once you mentally decide that you are a human being deserving of love- you take the first steps to regain your power! Pick up your strength and use it to thrive and flourish. It is indeed scary but what is and was even scarier, was thinking about when he succeeded in killing me, my children would either be a victim or become him. I could not have that. I needed to survive!

HIDDEN IN PLAIN SIGHT

I'm hiding
Behind an unknown mask
Afraid to see the real me
Fake. There is an entire cast

Who will accept this lonely heart?
Layers of active charcoal

Blackened flesh
I've never meshed
It's anyone's best guess
Unearth me
Uncover my truth
Expose me

Help me disassemble
My camouflaged trail
The cloak is my cover
Daunted to lift the veil

Can anyone see the real me?

Everything he said, "You're nothing," and me not amounting to
anything without him— was a lie. I did not need to hide anymore. I

am **SOMETHING**, I am **SOMEONE!** I am loved, worthy, healing, beautiful, and spiritually strong. I am Gabriella!

LOVE THYSELF

I love to be in love and have love surrounding me, it radiates off of me from

the inside out, my skin ablaze from its glow.

Love is embodied through me, within me, tantalizing the taste buds

that eat at the heart, blinded by a miry of colors;

darkness a distant memory of where love fills its place

dancing to the ballads of love, flowing in the air,

my fingers gliding across the aura of love,

and finally breathing in the scents of love.

Love is more tangible than credited but it starts with loving thyself

first.

Many years have passed since my marriage ended and I occasionally have to fight the tremors and terrors that came from those terrifying years. The children are older and are developing their own relationships with their father. Hearing his voice still brings me a level of discomfort that I am not sure will ever go away but I will no longer allow his manipulative ways affect how I maneuver through this life...

WHAT MY EARS HEARD

Today, I heard my abuser's voice for the first time in a decade.

I felt my body build an emotional wall of steel. I put on armor I had not put on in a long time.

It was not oiled for easy movement and I was stuck. Stuck trying to maneuver in the suit rather than being in fighting stance. I was struggling to fight... again!

God, where are You? Then, my ears heard another woman (his wife) tell me to get over my trauma. Those words transported me back to having my head bashed into an oven vent hood, the phone shook between my fingers as I grabbed my head. The pain instantly triggered by the memory.

Flashing lights happened behind my eyes like a movie screen. My eyes welled and my heart sank as the memories blurred one after the other. I tried willing my mind to make it stop but the force behind the movie reel was as powerful as the memory of my ex-husband's extra-large hands wrapped around my throat. I felt my throat tighten in the present, but I was taken back to the past gasping for air. The two circumstances merged into one. I felt dizzy in the present.

Rage engulfed me. My skin radiated with a fire that I was hell bent on putting out. I didn't want to feel this. I had no extinguisher. I didn't want to feel anything. I wanted to run.

Her words continued to taunt me... telling me to be quiet over my shouts, that it all happened in the past... "the past?", I screamed out. This is very real and current for me. My words drowned by past suffocation's.

In my ocean of tears, arms flailing to stay afloat. Too much water.... I can't see land. I'm scared of this place. I don't want to drown. Don't look down. Darkness lives there.

I can only look up; I force myself to. The sky is the most beautiful scenery. God is in the midst. My arms stop flailing, the water calms just as the Sea of Galilee. He called out to me, "Gabriella!" His hand appeared through the clouds. Peace be still, for I am with you. I will NEVER leave you nor forsake you. I reach for Him. A rainbow prism of light shines as our fingers meet and I'm brought back to 2020... alive, whole and well.

Theresa R. Simon

Executive Director & Founder of NDV Healing & Support Inc.

Website: https://ndvhealingsupportinc.org

NDV Facebook: https://www.facebook.com/NDVHealingSupport/

NDV Instagram: https://www.instagram.com/ndvhealingsupport/

NDV Twitter: https://twitter.com/HealingNdv

NDV Podcast: https://anchor.fm/ndvhealing

Theresa Simon, a domestic violence survivor of two abusive relationships, spent time focusing on healing, re-building her life after abuse, raising her children, and her career. During the phase of re-building her life after abuse, Theresa began a support group for domestic violence survivors, and later founded (and formed the support group into) the non-profit organization NDV (Narcissistic Domestic Violence) Healing and Support Inc., to assist victims of domestic violence, and provide education on domestic violence and narcissist abuse.

She is a motivational speaker, domestic violence advocate, and Podcast host. Theresa has over 10 years of experience in the case management/human services field, with state certified training. Theresa has assisted children and families as a Case Manager, Family Development Specialist, and Economic Support Specialist. Theresa continues to focus on her career, working in the Human Services/Social Services field, and has 11 classes (over 100 college credits completed) to finish her Bachelor of Arts in Criminal Justice (concentration in supervision and management). Theresa will continue on to obtain her graduate degree, in Criminal Justice, or law school.

Emerging from the Troubled Waters

It's the things that you least expect that hit you the hardest. *THWACK*! A searing sharp punch to my eye startles me and jolts me completely out of the seat. That statement has now taken on a different, more literal meaning. My eye is stinging, bleeding, my glasses are shattered and, on the ground; and I'm completely blindsided. There's a pressing and pulsating pain in my face and in my eye. *What the hell is happening?* He's screaming at me, as he attempts to grab the car keys and my cell phone. *"Where's your phone?"* He screams. My vision is blurred, I have no clue where my phone is at this point; it's temporarily lost due to the chaos, and to be honest I don't care where my phone is. I'm angry, confused, hurt, and now in pain. His screaming burns in my mind. I have just been punched in the face by my boyfriend, blindsided by the man who said he loved me, promised a life and kids with me and promised I was safe with him. I was picking up my purse not paying attention, when he blindsided me and punched me. Unbelievably, he punched me when I wasn't even looking.

"I don't know! I don't know where my phone is, I can't see it!" I shout back, my voice cracking as I yell. I'm trying to quickly lock the car doors and lock him out. Unfortunately, it doesn't work, I'm not fast enough, and he has already grabbed the car keys, my phone- now found again, and my purse. I realized I'm trapped. I'm trapped in this car with him. Have you ever felt like you are in a crowded room, screaming at the top of your lungs, but no one hears you or looks up?

Being trapped in this situation, this moment, feeling trapped in an abusive relationship, is quite like that. Feeling trapped, and overwhelmed by emotions, is the most accurate description of an abusive relationship.

"*Let's go!*" My boyfriend continues yelling. *Jason has taken my car keys, my cell phone, my purse, and is demanding I go upstairs to the apartment with him. *What choice do I have,* I think to myself? He has the car keys, my cell phone, and my purse. If I run, it's dark almost midnight. Where can I run to? There's no one around, and even worse I can't see out of my eye right now. I reluctantly follow him, walking along in the cold, dark night upstairs to the apartment. As we walk into the apartment building, I notice no one is around. It's desolate. We enter the apartment, and he ushers me to the bedroom. As I sit on the bed stunned, Jason comes back from the kitchen with ice for my face. As I place the ice to my face, unable to open my eye, he is still upset and yelling and grabs my phone. Jason looks angrily as he scrolls through my phone again, looking through my text messages, social media, and call logs. I sit quietly on the bed holding the cold ice to my face.

" *Who is this?*" He asks. He is reading my text messages. There is a social media message from a male co-worker asking me about work and inquiring about the voluntary time off management has been giving at work. I can see now that he is going to misconstrue anything he sees, to make it appear like I'm trying to talk to another man. I have been faithful this entire relationship, but at the time I didn't know I was dealing with a narcissist, and that facts wouldn't matter.

"It's a co-worker asking me a question about work, that's all." I said quietly responding to Jason.

"You are in a relationship!" Jason yells at me, as he paces back and forth in the bedroom. He hits me again, hitting the side of my head, not nearly as hard, but I drop the ice I was holding for my eye. I pick up the ice, and stare out of the window, thinking. My thoughts are racing. Jason sits back down in the old recliner next to the bed, seething with anger. The room goes quiet for a while, dead silence, as he continues to rummage through my cell phone. In the silence, my thoughts are racing as I contemplate leaving. *How would I get out of the bedroom,* I think? There is only one way out of the bedroom, and if I made it out of the bedroom, there is only one way out of the apartment. *I could leave when he goes to sleep, but how long will that be?*

Satisfied he has gone through everything in my phone, Jason takes my cell phone and hides it in the next room. He comes back into the bedroom and takes a seat again in the old recliner, it creaks as he sits down. I haven't moved from the same spot. I'm frozen. I'm wondering how long it will take for him to calm down, but I know the answer to that. It will be hours, before he calms down. I think to myself; *I haven't done anything wrong. I haven't cheated, I haven't talked to any man, or gone anywhere except for the house, and work, why is he so upset,* I think. I realize he has demons tormenting him, things he is fighting within himself, that really have nothing to do with money, or him looking in my phone to find something that isn't there. The demons he is fighting have nothing to do with me at all.

I sit quietly as Jason picks up his favorite bottle of cognac and continues drinking. Hours passed, which seemed like years, and he is now calm. Jason continues to drink, and quietly sit in the recliner. It's astonishing to watch how he can go from a fit of range, demanding things be a certain way, to calm, cool, and loving. It seems to be two different people, each with distinct personalities. There is the calm, cool, charming, loving Jason, and then there is the cold enraged Jason. You never know which Jason you will get. He can change like a flip of a light switch, and without warning. I have now gotten ready for bed, as I realize it's very late, and there is no way I can really leave to go anywhere.

At this point, I have no idea, where my cell phone, car keys, or purse is inside of the apartment anyhow. I'm exhausted, emotionally drained, and in physical pain. Jason has hidden my stuff anyway, to ensure I will not leave. I start to lay down in the bed, and get comfortable, as comfortable as I can with my face starting to swell. Fatigued, Jason climbs into bed next to me and begins to hold me. Normally, he does hold me at night (while we are sleeping or I'm laying on him). It's our routine. This is different, he has just punched me in my face. He appears to be remorseful, so I let him hold me. It's difficult to comprehend how a person can go from what seems like two different people. I'm hurt, but mostly I'm bewildered. There is a huge part of me, that wants nothing to do with him, but there's that other part of me, that still loves him. I have so many emotions running through me at this very moment, that it's overwhelming. I am not sure what to do or feel, as I am becoming overwhelmed with emotions.

Jason begins to kiss me and rub sensually and softly on my body. I let out a sigh. Jason also lets out a sigh. He wants to be intimate with me. I can tell that Jason wants to have sex. I'm still very angry with him, and I still have a swollen face. I also still love him. I also want to be intimate with him, too. I'm completely perplexed.

Domestic violence is not as black and white, or cut and dry as people seem to think it is. Domestic violence is not a one size fits all, situation. Domestic violence is a unique experience, for each survivor. It's not just your intimate partner physically assaults you; you defend yourself or not, and the police are called; it's much more than that. Domestic violence is a truly complex web that includes, physical, emotional, psychological, financial, sexual, narcissist, and a traumatic bond.

The traumatic bond is something that countless people do not understand, and something that took me awhile to comprehend myself. This traumatic bond is difficult to break. A trauma bond (also known as Stockholm Syndrome) is a type of toxic bond that occurs when the abuser alternates between creating highs and lows within the relationship, with the intermittent reinforcement of reward and punishment. Thus, cycles of abuse are followed by intermittent love or reward; leaving the victim craving comfort from the very person who hurt them. The trauma bond is an addiction like alcoholism, that can be difficult to break, and you go through withdrawal and relapses.

Trauma bonds usually occur or form in childhood or as a result of unresolved past trauma. The traumatic bond, the addiction, is why many find it difficult to leave abusive relationships. It is also the reason that many people struggle with their relationships with their parents, as the traumatic bond is complex. I think to myself, as Jason continues to kiss me, *how did I get here? How did I get into this relationship; how am I at this point?* Those insightful questions are definitely questions to ponder.

Growing up, I was raised by my mother. I grew up in a single parent household. My parents were married almost eighteen years, and my parents divorced when I was in second grade. Life was uneventful most days, and I lived with my mother and my older sister. My sister is seven years older than me, and would babysit me, and pick me up from school. I was a typical bratty younger sister. I grew up in Waukegan, Illinois, a large suburb approximately 45 minutes north of Chicago, Illinois. My family and I lived in a relatively quiet neighborhood in Waukegan, with a lot of children in the area. I often rode bikes or played outside with the neighborhood children. For the most part a seemingly typical childhood.

As I grew older, the late elementary school years, I realized that something was off. I knew something wasn't right, but I wasn't sure what it was. I couldn't put my finger on it; that revelation of what was really happening would not come until I was much older. It was a nagging feeling, producing anxiety in me. I was anxious often, and I struggled with my anxiety throughout my younger years. Although, my parents were divorced and I lived with my mother, I would see my dad. However, I did not see my dad every weekend. I saw my dad sporadically, and during special events, birthdays, holidays, and some major school events. My dad remarried, during my late elementary school years, to my stepmother, *Dalia. This is when I knew there was a change, a shift in my life, but again I couldn't quite comprehend what was taking place, at this time. I was too young, to fully grasp it all.

My stepmother made it painfully clear that she did not want my father, to have a relationship with his children. My stepmother had a daughter, * Sara, who was two years older than me. Dalia wanted my father to treat her child as his child, and just "erase" his children. I still visited my dad when I was in elementary, and up until early middle school. When I would visit my dad, I would play with Sara sometimes. However, if anything happened in the house, it was always my fault. Sara was never blamed for anything. I was always the scapegoat. I grew up to become the scapegoat in my family, which was painfully clear in my adult years, by being left by my family the night before my sister's wedding. My outspoken, strong-willed personality was fuel to the fire.

Nonetheless, I always stood up for myself, even if I was the only one standing up for me. However, it's exhausting to always defend yourself. It's exhausting to feel like you are on your own emotionally, and worse, that people don't believe in you. If you are the family scapegoat, your character is attacked, while around your family, and publicly when you are not around. The scapegoat is usually the outspoken, blatantly honest person who does not sweep the family issues under the rug, which is met with being treated negatively by family members, as they do not want to confront the family issues, or dysfunction, by rather place blame on scapegoat for any issues. A perfect example of scapegoat treatment, in my adult years, not only did my family leave me and drove off in the van the night before my sister's wedding, but once I arrived at the wedding my character was already attacked. I arrived at the wedding, after my family drove off in the van, only to have people believe that I was out to sabotage my sister's wedding, because I would not attend. How ridiculous, that I would be accused of sabotaging a wedding, when I was trying to get in the van, and was not allowed into the van. Not one person in my family stood up for me and said, "*hey we should let her in the van*". Not one person stood up, and said, "*hey she wasn't trying to sabotage a wedding, we didn't let her in the van.*"

Like I said, I've always had a thick skin, thankfully, and most things didn't get to me, but one thing that always seem to get to me, was being the scapegoat in my family. It would later take its toll, as I struggled to break the trauma bond with my family, to the trauma bond with my second abusive relationship.

Dalia made sure that there were issues between my father and his children. Sara once complained I was teasing her too much (as children often do with each other), and I was screamed at. As I grew older, the visits to my dad's house, were less and less, until they were almost nonexistent. By the time I reached late middle school, the visits had ceased, except for holidays. Dalia's erasing of my father's children had taken place, as she wanted.

During the middle school years, I dealt with the typical adolescent struggles, with fitting in, making friends, and finding your way. I was an intelligent, articulate child, but did not hang out with the bookworm crowd, and I had a lot of friends. Thus, I would say I was semi-popular. I was outspoken, outgoing, and although I was still trying to make sense of my relationship with my parents, I was confident. I definitely wasn't a push over, or easily shattered. I was, and still am, an alpha female. I made a lot of friends, who understood these various sides of me (as we all have different sides to us), but there were also people who didn't. As with most adolescents, there were those in school who mistook the confidence and outspokenness for being too outspoken, or too articulate.

Despite what was going on in my home life, and the inconsistent (trauma) bond with my parents, I had a pretty thick skin, especially towards the outside world. Being the scapegoat in my family, it forced me to have a thick skin. Having a thick skin, I think bothered those who didn't like me even more. As late middle school went on, those who did not like me, decided to make up rumors about me and tease me. Typical adolescent behavior, I always stood up for myself. I wasn't the type to sit there quietly or let someone talk about me while staying silent.

However, the rumors and teasing followed into high school like an annoying fly you can't get rid of; and I continued to ignore those who lied about me, didn't like me, or had made up issues with me, unless confronted directly. I lived by the motto, opinions aren't facts, and you don't concern yourself with what people think of you. I was less bothered by some of the kids at school that didn't like me, and more bothered by what was going on with my father and my family life. As I settled into a very busy high school life, I became very focused on my schoolwork, almost obsessed in some respects. I began to excel academically, and in other areas. My goal was to become a criminal defense attorney, and for many years this was my goal. I loved law, and I wanted to make a difference in the criminal justice system. I love helping people. As an empath, it's what I excel at. I was in the College Studies Program and honors classes in high school. I also joined the cheerleading team, JROTC, student council, and other clubs. I also worked part-time during high school. I made more friends in the different clubs I was a part of, and I continued to focus on what I wanted to do after high school. Most of my time I concentrated on college, and overall enjoyed my last years of high school, being semi-popular, and time with my friends.

During this time in high school, I would still only go to my father's house during holidays. At my dad's house during the holidays, I would observe that there would always be more (money or presents) given to Sara than my sister and me. If Sara needed something, for example shoes or winter coat, it was given without question. If I needed something or my sister, it was difficult to get it, and if we did eventually get it, it was always made to seem like my father had to sneak to give it to us. In some cases, my father did sneak and get us things we needed. It was considered sneaking because

Dalia did not know and did not want my father to spend money on his children. It was expected that my mother was to provide the things we need, which she did, but both parents are to provide for their children.

I graduated high school after completing four years in the College Studies Program and moved into my dorm at Michigan State University, Yakeley Gilchrist Hall. I was ready to begin my career as a criminal defense attorney, and I was majoring in criminal justice. I was a traditional college student, and explored Michigan, as I hadn't visited Michigan much prior to living there. I made a lot of new friends in Michigan and learned a lot about myself during this period. I spent a lot of time on campus, learning my new surroundings. Just like with high school, I was making new friends, focusing on my schoolwork, joining clubs, working, and having an eventful and demanding life. Still, something was off, and I still couldn't figure out exactly what it was.

Have you ever felt a nagging feeling, that won't go away? I'm in my early 20's, away from home in college at Michigan State University, meeting new people, having the time of my life, just like my high school years. I'm living what is the best years of your life, yet I have feelings of anxiety and a nagging feeling that something is off. A feeling that I can't seem to shake.

I would sometimes come home during holiday breaks. I would alternate between going home during holiday breaks or staying at my friends' houses in Michigan. During a break from school, while at home, I decided to go out with my sister and her friends. *It's ladies' night, but it's not the bar I would have chosen*, I say to myself as I look around. Still, I came here to have fun, so I take a seat by the bar.

I sit down and I'm surveying the room when a tall well-dressed man casually approaches me. I didn't know it at the time, but I had just met the father of my children. It's interesting how a chance meeting, can drastically change the course of your life.

I later would find out, that several people I knew, knew him, I just didn't. He asked me the basic questions, (what's your name, how old are you) attempting to get to know me, and I'm listening to him talk. I barely touched my drink, as he leaned in as he speaks to me. The bar is noisy and it's difficult to hear. I could tell he's older than me, and he seemed to escape answers to some of my questions. Nonetheless, he was funny, and slightly entertaining, and I like funny. I'm intrigued.

*Brandon asks for my phone number, as I get ready to leave the club with my sister and friends. I reluctantly give my number, as that nagging feeling comes back again. I ignore the feeling and give him my number. *What could it hurt*, I thought? I would soon find the answer to that question.

Brandon and I began talking more on the phone, and began going out on dates, and getting to know each other. The relationship was moving very quickly, but I felt more like a passenger along for a ride, than an active participant at times. I was young, and hadn't had many relationships, so I was naïve. Nonetheless, the break was coming to a close, and it was time to return to school to start the next semester. I made a drastic decision that would change the course of my life.

I decided to take a break, and not return for the next semester. I decided to take a semester off, return home, and work for a retail company. I thought, plenty of people take breaks from college, and return. I know that I'll still get my degree, I thought. My plan was to return to Michigan State University, the following semester, and return to my normal schedule. During the break, I began to spend more time with Brandon. The relationship progresses and we continue dating. As I started to get to know him, red flags began to emerge. There were never real answers to my questions, I would ask him. Brandon was always evasive with answers. He was extremely evasive, because he did not want me to find out the truth about who he really was. I later learned in order to reel me in, he lied about several things. Brandon lied about how many children he had. He also lied about his employment. Brandon had spurts of employment, but never stayed on a job for a long period of time. I later found out, that he would move from job to job.

Considering that Brandon was almost seven years older than me, I started to see how unstable his life was. Brandon discussed his ex-girlfriend, making her out to be a villain, but he conveniently would leave out what he had done to make her so angry. Brandon also conveniently left out that he still talked with her, and even worse that was not all that he was not honest about. In fact, those red flags, were just the tip of the iceberg, I would later find out.

I stayed with Brandon, thinking that at any moment, I could just leave. This won't be serious. I can leave this relationship, at any time. The right moment to leave was now, but I kept telling myself I would walk away soon. However, soon never came. I continued working my retail job and began preparing for my return to Michigan. I felt like returning to Michigan would be a good way to end this relationship. Brandon was not who he said he was, and he was not the type of man I wanted to be with. I wanted to be with someone who was hard working, ambitious, goal driven, honest, and Brandon was not any of those things. Brandon was moving along the relationship rather quickly, love bombing me, and I felt like now would be a good time to break away from this.

I was ready to get back to Michigan, and back to my life. I missed Michigan, and I missed the college campus at this point. I missed the stores I frequented on Grand River Avenue, next to the MSU campus. I missed my normal routine, and my life as a traditional college student. I missed my friends, the crisp weather as I walked along the idyllic campus. As I prepared for my return to Michigan, I received alarming news. I discovered I was pregnant. I was stunned, but more concerned about having to raise a child with Brandon. I felt trapped, like I now had to be with Brandon. I felt compelled to make the best of this relationship, knowing deep down the relationship wasn't what I truly wanted. I knew I always wanted to be a mother, but I pictured being a mother, after I had graduated law school, and after I was married. However, life takes detours, and it's fine, because you can still reach your destination and your goals. The plot in the story of your life changes; you may go back, ponder and re-read some of the chapters, but you'll find out that you are responsible for creating your own adventure. You are one decision away from having the life you really want. No matter how many detours you encounter, and no matter how long it takes you, you can still reach your ultimate destination.

I decided to wait until after our daughter was born to return to Michigan. It was during my pregnancy, that the real Brandon came out. The love bombing stage, was over. All of Brandon's dark secrets he had been hiding came out, and I realized who he really was. Brandon became emotionally abusive and controlling. It was Brandon's way or the highway. Brandon was no longer working either, and it appeared he didn't really have a plan for what he wanted to do with his life. I felt like I was on a roll coaster ride, that I no longer wanted to be on. Brandon would call me incessantly if I was at work, or not around him, but when I was available, he would be out cheating, I learned.

My pregnancy was progressing It was not an easy one due to all the stress and emotional abuse I was enduring from Brandon. I was becoming physically sick, mostly due to the stress I was under. Brandon did not start to physically abuse me, until I was pregnant. One in six women that are abused, are abused first during pregnancy. The first time he physically assaulted me, the first time I had ever been physically assaulted in my life, was when I was pregnant, and he threw me through the apartment wall. I stood there in disbelief, trapped in the sparsely decorated bedroom. There was a gaping hole in the drywall, and as if that wasn't enough, he began strangling me.

Domestic abuse victims are ten times more likely to be killed if suspects strangled them or have strangled them previously. Thus, strangulation is a substantial indicator of homicide, and something to be taken very seriously. I couldn't breathe and I blacked out. I came to, in the same spot on the bed. I was stunned, almost frozen. I couldn't believe that this was happening. I felt like I was in the Twilight Zone. He pretended to be remorseful but moved on as if it was no big deal. Brandon acted as if it was no big deal, and that next time I should just listen to him. After making dinner that night, Brandon began cuddling with me, as if everything was alright. I lay there, still in a state of shock, and not to mention pain.

The frequency of physical abuse continued throughout the pregnancy. There was an incident where Brandon was sitting at the kitchen table, cutting up food, and holding the knife, looking at me, daring me to walk out the door. Brandon had informed me that I was not leaving, which was something he did often, tell me that I was not able to leave.

However, the most horrific incident occurred when I was five, almost six months pregnant. Brandon and I were laying in bed, and he had just been rude and had an attitude. This behavior is typical of narcissistic abusers. I decided I had enough of him being emotionally abusive, and I was tired, so I decided to just leave, and I would come back later. Brandon decided he wanted to have sex. *Is he crazy*, I thought? He's being emotionally abusive and wants me to have sex. I told him I was leaving, and I would not be having sex with him. *This is ridiculous*, I thought.

Before I can get out anymore words, Brandon hurriedly grabs me, and throws me on the bed. He punches me in the face, but at the last minute I turn my head, so the punch hits my ear. *I must get out of here*, I tell myself. My ear is ringing, and I hear and feel, a pop in my ear. I know there is some damage to my ear, but right now that's the least of my concerns. Brandon is hitting me and telling me that he wants to have sex, that he "has to finish." Brandon "finishes," as I maintained that I did not want to have sex. He's calm afterwards, and wants to cuddle, but I don't want to cuddle. I don't even want to speak to him or look at him. I'm disgusted with him, and I want to leave. I know if I leave or run out, it will cause him to get upset, and try to prevent me from leaving. Thus, I will wait to leave as he calms down, I thought. Brandon starts to get ready for bed, and I tell him I must go to the store for a few items. I get up the stairs, and once outside, I bolt to my car. I am not ever coming back I tell myself.

I'm driving down the dark road. It's raining as I sit at the stop light. My ear is throbbing, and I know I need to go to the hospital to see if I'm okay. Also, I want to make sure the baby is okay, too. This would be the first time I have ever gone to the hospital. I have never reported abuse before. Reluctantly, I decided I needed to go to the hospital to at least have a checkup, to make sure everything was alright.

I arrive at the only hospital in the area, worried and nervous. I'm not sure what to expect. I tell them that I am pregnant, and I tell them what has happened to me. I've been beaten by boyfriend. I tell them my ear feels uncomfortable. The physician checks my ears, and does an ultrasound, just to be on the safe side. The baby is fine, I'm told, as I breathe a sigh of relief. My ear, however, is not. I had a perforated eardrum. I would have to be careful and let it heal, and make sure nothing got inside my ear. I would have to come back to the doctor in a few weeks to have my ear checked again. As I'm getting ready to get discharged from the hospital, the police arrived. The hospital called the police, which is standard practice in most areas, but at the time, I didn't know that.

The police began asking me questions about what took place. I don't really want to talk to the police at this moment. I'm exhausted, emotionally drained, in pain, and I just want to lay down. I don't feel comfortable talking to a man I don't know and explaining what happened. Brandon is going to be furious if he finds out I went to the hospital and the police were called.

A warrant is placed out for Brandon's arrest. Before Brandon is arrested, Brandon decided to leave the state for a little while so that he would not get arrested. Brandon wanted me to come with him. I decided that I didn't want to go out of state with him. Half of me was hoping this was my break, my way to get away from him, finally. The other half of me, was still confused. I had made my decision; I was not going to leave with Brandon. This was going to be it.

In August 2005, after an emergency cesarean section due to preeclampsia, our beautiful daughter was born. I couldn't have been more excited to be a mother. She was finally here, after what seemed like the longest pregnancy ever. After eight weeks, I returned to working retail preparing for my return to Michigan in January. I planned to return to Michigan in January 2006 for the spring semester at Michigan State University. I was going to bring my daughter and her and I would live on campus, in the Cherry Lane campus apartments. Brandon had returned from out of state, and I was seeing him, but still trying to slowly break free. Brandon and I talked during this time, and he visited but I continued to make strides to move forward.

Finally, January 2006 came, and I moved into the Cherry Lane campus apartments at Michigan State University, with my daughter. I began settling into my new life as a college student, and new mom. I was determined to finish my bachelor's degree, so that I could finally start law school, and get started in a new career. I was also glad I was out of state and away from Brandon. It was a new start for me, and my daughter. Finally, it felt like I was putting this abusive relationship behind me. I was ready to focus on my daughter and new law career.

Statistically on average it takes seven attempts to leave an abusive relationship. This wasn't going to be an easy task. Brandon came to visit me and our new daughter while I was at Michigan State University. I could feel myself getting sucked back in, again. When Brandon wasn't visiting, he made sure he called frequently. I also came home during some weekends, so that my family could spend time with my daughter.

The end of spring semester at MSU finally came, and I was preparing to move out of campus apartments and return in the fall. My daughter was now six months old. I noticed I hadn't been feeling very well lately, and I attributed it to the demands of being a new mom, and college student. Still, I decided to go to the doctor, as my intuition is usually right. My intuition was telling me that I wasn't just sick. I went to the doctor, and found out, while I had a six-month-old baby, I'm now also pregnant. I wasn't concerned about telling Brandon. I was sure that would go fine. I was more concerned with how I was going to raise two children so close in age, and finish college, and work. I also was concerned with how this would play out with Brandon. I was trying not to get sucked back in, and yet here I was getting further sucked in.

I knew by fall I would be very close to giving birth, so it was now likely, if I returned to MSU after my move home, I would have to go back for the Spring Semester instead. I gave birth to a son in December 2006. After the birth of my son, I began transitioning from working in retail to customer service. I would later give birth to my third child with Brandon, a daughter, in December 2008.

Six and half years of this on and off abusive relationship and 3 kids later, I was determined to leave for good this time. This wasn't a healthy relationship, and although my kids were babies, I didn't want them to see unhealthy relationships. I wanted better for my kids.

In December 2009, I walked away from my abusive relationship with Brandon and never looked back. I had reached a point where I was really fed up, and there wasn't really a strong trauma bond there, by the time I left. It was more of an obligation, I felt at times, because he was the father of my three children. There comes a time, where you just reach the point where enough is enough. I no longer wanted to be a part of this relationship anymore, and I was fed up with Brandon's lying and cheating. I was determined to get my track, the way I envisioned it would be many years before meeting him.

I spent the next ten years healing, focusing on raising my children, my career, and my goals. At this time, I didn't go to therapy, because I mistakenly thought I could navigate the healing process on my own, without therapy or coaching. Once again, like when I was in high school and I immersed myself in schoolwork, I immersed myself in my new career. I began my career in the human services field, and I have over ten years of experience in the case management/human services field with state certified training. I have assisted children and families as a Case Manager, Family Development Specialist, and Economic Support Specialist.

I was preparing to later make my career transition from human services to law, as I initially wanted to do. I had two (non-abusive) relationships during that time. As I started this new career path though, I stayed out of relationships for over a year as I focused on my children. My children were excelling in their new school, and life was pretty good. I had a three-bedroom townhouse, and I felt like the children and I were doing well.

Now, I felt like I was ready to date again. Everything in my life, was starting to fall into place. I felt like I was ready for another serious relationship or so I thought. Now was a good time. The relationship started off well, but once again, I found myself in another abusive relationship with a narcissist. I met Jason in January 2019. Jason and I had attended the same middle school, and high school. Jason and I had the same associates, or knew a large amount of the same people, so I knew who Jason was, I just never spoke much to him. Jason was handsome, charming, and charismatic. However, I was older now, in my 30's, and I wanted a man who was hard working, ambitious, goal driven, honest, and an excellent father. He had to be much more than just charming and charismatic. I knew exactly what type of man I wanted, and what I wanted out of a relationship.

Jason was working as a forklift driver when I met him, and he was able to hold down a job. In fact, Jason worked six out of seven days a week. Jason also visited with his kids throughout the week and talked to them on the phone often. He made sure he brought his mother groceries, hoped to make supervisor, and had plans to open his own business one day. Jason opened up to me about his childhood, traumatic events that happened in his life. It looked like I had found the attributes I was looking for in a man. It appeared that I found a soulmate. We connected and had several similarities. We spent a lot of time together, and when we weren't together or we were at work, we were on the phone with each other. I didn't know it at the time, but I was being love bombed by Jason.

Narcissistic abuse includes the terms love bombing, trauma bond, gaslighting, hovering, projecting, chaos bombing, and triangulation. Narcissistic abuse consists of the stages of idealization, devaluation, and discard. Love bombing occurs during the idealization phase of narcissistic abuse. Love bombing is when a narcissist overwhelms you with actions, words, attention, and loving behavior, to manipulate you. The narcissists' love is based on your loyalty, and what you can do for them. The narcissist will gain your trust, and obtain affection from you, in order to establish a trauma bond, so that it will make it difficult for you to leave, and so that they can control you.

Jason was more emotionally abusive than physically abusive. (Whereas, Brandon was more physically abusive than emotionally abusive.) Jason was emotionally abusive, and controlling, but not in the presence of others. Jason had to appear charming and charismatic when others were around us. There were two physically abusive incidents during my relationship with Jason, and countless times I experienced emotional and financial abuse. Jason was never sexually abusive, however.

In August 2019, the first physical abusive incident, Jason strangled me. He was being verbally abusive that night. I was already distraught because it was the week of my sister's wedding and my family took off in the van and left me before the wedding. My sister was having a destination wedding in Louisiana, and we all chipped in, to pay to rent a van, so that we would all drive to my sister's wedding together. A family member decided that because I was in abusive relationship, I needed to be a "better mother," and would not let me in the van. The family member was attempting tough love. However, you cannot tough love someone out of an abusive relationship, especially if they are trauma bonded. This is a myth. The trauma bond is an addiction, and tough love will not help the victim break the trauma bond.

No one in my family, not one person, stepped up to say I should be let into the van. I had to rent a car and drive over fourteen hours by myself to get to the wedding, myself. I knew I was the family scapegoat, but leaving me before the wedding, was unforgiveable. It was a new low. Again, once I arrived at the wedding, the narrative was being pushed, that I was trying to sabotage the wedding. They neglected to mention the circumstances that led to my being late. The narrative (due to being a scapegoat) was always pushed that Theresa is trying to ruin something, whether it's something of my families' (an event), or my own life. Theresa is always guilty of or doing something.

As I said, I was distraught about my family taking off in the van and leaving me, and Jason had been drinking heavily that night. I knew when I pulled up, he was drunk, and I thought to myself this wasn't going to be a good night. I was hoping that Jason would understand how distraught I was, and he would not be in one of his "moods." Jason appeared to be sympathetic initially to what happened with my family, but as the night went on, and Jason continued to drink, Jason's attitude changed. Like the flip of a light switch, the "other" personality comes out again. Jason became angry and agitated, continuing to drink. Jason wanted to get his car out of the shop, and he was mad because I "had" to give him the money to do it. He put his car in the shop to get it painted, and detailed (not necessary, not necessary, at least not necessary to get him to work), and I should pay for it. I had already given him money for that, but he blew it on alcohol/ drinking, and other unimportant miscellaneous things, so he wanted more money. Jason was also upset that I was going out of town, to Louisiana to my sister's wedding. He felt like I should stay with him, and what was the point, my family had left me. Jason became emotionally and verbally abusive, and I decided that I had had enough. I am already distraught because my family left me. I wasn't in the mood to deal with much else. I began to put my shoes on and grab my car keys and phone.

"*Where are you going?*" Jason asked irritated, standing up now.

"*I'm leaving. I don't have time for this,*" I snapped back. As soon as I said the words, Jason picked me up and slammed me onto the bed. Jason began strangling me. I'm struggling to breathe, and there is nothing around me to hit him with to get him off me. His weight and pressure are almost too much, but finally he lets go. My neck is sore, and it almost feels like I can't talk. Jason has never hit me before. He was emotionally abusive, controlling, and he yelled at me, but never had he put his hands on me. In fact, he always promised me I was safe with him, and that would never happen. I guess that was one of his many lies.

I continued to stay with Jason after that, hoping that would be the first and last physically abusive incident. The emotional abuse was not okay either, but I kept hoping that Jason would be the man he was in the beginning. I didn't fully grasp at the time, that Jason was a narcissist who was love bombing me, and the man I met at the beginning of the relationship did not really exist.

A few months later, in November 2019, Jason was dealt a devastating blow, when a close family member died unexpectedly. Jason's family member was in the hospital in the Intensive Care Unit for a week, and Jason struggled to deal with this. Our relationship was still rocky as Jason was still emotionally abusive, but during this time, I knew he needed someone to be there for him. I loved him, and despite everything I didn't want to see him hurt. Instead of walking away, I stayed with him. I went to the hospital with him. After a week, the family member passed away. I knew Jason was hurting and I was there for him. We had a period, "the honeymoon period" of the abuse cycle, where Jason was the man, I met in the beginning, loving, caring, and sweet. He was love bombing again, of course. As with all honeymoon phases of the abuse cycle, it was short lived.

The second and final physically abusive incident, with Jason, happened November 27, 2019, the night before Thanksgiving. Jason first took me to the gas station, to withdraw money out of my account. A check cleared my account, that I didn't think was going to clear yet, so there wasn't a lot of money in my account. The check had just cleared, so now I had to tell him, there wasn't enough money in the account, as we left the gas station, and he lost it. We pulled up to his apartment building, and while we were in the car, he punched me in my face. I was looking for the items that fell out of purse, since he threw my purse around, so I wasn't looking at him when he punched me. I was completely blindsided.

The person who told me he loved me, and promised to keep me safe, said we would have a son one day, and get married, punches me in my face. I was devasted and in disbelief. Remember, Jason then began going through my phone, text messages, social media, and pictures, to determine if I was cheating, which I'm sure he knew I wasn't cheating. It was a way to continue to control me, but meanwhile he is going through my phone, and I am sitting here with a black eye and in pain.

It's unreal when the person who supposed to love and protect you, punches you in the face. Jason took my phone, purse and car keys, and I had no access to my things, or no way to leave that night. Jason demanded I go upstairs with him into the apartment. I am now trapped, with someone and I'm not even sure what he will do next. He sent text messages to my kids, pretending to be me, so they won't worry why I haven't called them yet, and why I'm not answering my phone. My kids know this is not like me, and they were worried sick anyway. The next day when I was finally given my car keys, phone, and purse, I first went to the hospital, to have them check on my eye. Afterwards I went home because I knew my kids were worried. When my children saw my face, they were horrified, to see the black eye. My kids had never experienced anything like that. They had never experienced or witnessed abuse, as I left their father when they were babies. Not only did my children have to move due to the financial abuse, but now they saw their mother with a black eye. The abuse didn't just affect me, it affected my children, also. I never wanted my children to hurt.

Also, I had to have several days off work because my glasses were on when he punched me, and the glasses shattered and scratched my eye. The scratch or cut on my eye was painful. I was unable to be around lights for several days. The doctor gave me prescription eye drops that eased the pain, so that I could see comfortably, and be able to be around lights, as my job, has huge bright lights in the office.

As the trauma bond was very strong, I stayed with Jason after he punched me in the face. The following day was Thanksgiving, and the day after we still spent the holiday together. The weekend of the holiday, Jason and I went to hang out over at his friend's house, as we often did. I put a lot of makeup over my black eye, but it was still noticeable. I believed people noticed but didn't want to say anything; it's the elephant in the room. Jason doted on me as usual, fixing my drink and my food, and cuddling up next to me. I knew that this was only going to last so long. Soon the "other side" of Jason, was going to come out again, and it was only a matter of time.

The following day, the other side of Jason came back again. He was verbally abusive and yelling again. It was at that very moment, I decided I couldn't do this anymore. Every abuse victim gets to the point, where they decide this is it. My final straw was that day. I'm sitting here with a black eye, and he's yelling at me again, about something trivial as usual. I couldn't do this anymore. I was done.

I stopped answering his text messages and phone calls. I went to get a restraining order, and there was a warrant out for his arrest, one for previous charges unrelated to me, and one for the assault on me. I was trying to put my life back together. I also just moved into a new place. It was time to take my life back, and continue to focus on my children, and my career, and not look back. Only this time, I would really heal, I vowed.

January 2020, Jason was arrested for his assault on me. Our relationship was officially over. I was reeling from the trauma bond, and I decided for the first time, to finally begin therapy. Through therapy, and education on domestic violence and narcissist abuse, I began to finally heal. I finally began to do the work. In order to come out on the other side, and cross that bridge, you must do the work. After my first abusive relationship, I didn't do the work. I didn't go to counseling or coaching. I decided this time, I was ready to do the work. That nagging feeling that wouldn't go away and kept giving me anxiety, throughout the stages of my life. I learned through therapy and education that it was due to being a scapegoat in the family. Once I learned about the different dysfunctional family roles, such as scapegoat, golden child, etc. I learned the feeling that was nagging at me all these years, was the hurt and trauma.

My family leaving me and taking off in the van only solidified that feeling. Finally, I realized that whatever narrative someone is pushing about you (especially being the scapegoat), you don't have to accept that narrative. It doesn't matter if someone else is not proud of you or doesn't love you. I love me, and that's enough. I am proud of me, of all I've overcome, and all that I will do. It took me years to finally get to this point, but I'm not done yet. There's so much more I want to do. There's so much more I want to conquer.

I began an online support group for women who have experienced domestic violence, which really blossomed. NDV Healing and Support Inc. (Narcissistic Domestic Violence) initially began as a support group and officially became a non-profit organization 501 (c) (3), March 3, 2020. NDV Healing and Support Inc. provides premier services for domestic violence victims (women and their children), including mentoring and coaching, domestic violence/narcissist abuse education, and promotes domestic violence awareness throughout the community.

NDV Healing and Support Inc. provides a wide range of services for domestic violence survivors, and has an engaging and informative podcast called, NDV Healing. I continue to focus on my career, working in the Human Services/Social Services field, Executive Director for NDV Healing and Support Inc., and I have 11 classes (over 100 college credits completed) to finish my Bachelor of Arts in Criminal Justice (concentration in supervision and management). I will continue to obtain my graduate degree, in Criminal Justice or attend law school. I also want to eventually obtain my PHD. I will never give up on myself.

I want my pain to become someone else's map. I'm passionate about helping other women thrive and get through their journey. I survived domestic violence/narcissist abuse, and I want you to know you can, as well. The traumatic bond (addiction) is challenging to break, but not impossible. It can be difficult to leave, but you can do it. You will have to work every day, to get through the trauma bond and stay no contact with the abuser. I want domestic violence/narcissist abuse survivors to know this: 1) that you are not alone, 2) you are not what happened to you, 3) It's not your fault, and 4) you can overcome this and rebuild your life. You don't just wake up and become the butterfly. Growth is a process. Healing is also a process, and not linear. You cannot emerge from the troubled waters, without first learning to fight and swim through them. You will learn to rise above the storm.

Dr. Stacy L. Henderson-Shaw

P. O. Box 886913

Great Lakes, IL 60088-6913

drstacylhenderson@gmail.com

Dr. Stacy L. Henderson-Shaw, a native of Savannah, Georgia, is a highly decorated retired Naval Officer with over 25 years of military service and experience. She is a Christian Educator, Inspirational Speaker, Businesswoman and an International Best-Selling Author. She speaks four languages and has publications in more than 40 language translations - two of which are in the White House Library. She is currently the Senior Naval Science Instructor (SNSI), at a Chicago-Suburbs High School, where she is the first African-American and the first woman to hold the position. Her *Stacy's Stocking Stuffers* Christmas Charity has provided toys, meals, coats, clothing and monetary support for families around the world since 1991.

Stacy has spent most of her life overcoming challenges. Her *'Survival Journal'* chronicles her trauma and triumph over childhood sexual assault and domestic abuse as an adult. She shares first-hand accounts while raising awareness of domestic violence. *'Fair Winds And Following Seas'* is a letter written to her Navy Shipmates during the recovery and rehabilitation process after a near fatal domestic incident. The letter was later recreated as a Public Service Announcement (MarcMann Productions, Chicago) and is widely used in Military Domestic Violence training sessions.

Her other military-themed PSAs based on her experiences include: *'Introducing Stacy L. Henderson: The Woman Behind the Uniform'*; *'The Sailor on the Pier'* and *'The War At Home.'*

Her personal story of triumph over tragedy was featured in Military One Source Magazine, Great Lakes Bulletin and multiple other Military Magazines. An active Member of the National Coalition Against Domestic Violence, Stacy is an avid supporter of abuse victims, survivors, and their loved ones and still supports the programs at the Shelter where she and her children once resided. The facility was instrumental in their safe escape from an abusive environment. With violence on the rise among our youth, she also provides age-appropriate anti-bullying training to young adults. She testified at Congressional Hearings in efforts to get tougher abuse perpetrator laws passed during the President Clinton and President Obama Administrations (Violence Against Women Act).

Stacy has worked on projects with Paramount Motion Pictures, *Lifetime* Television, BET, TV One, Mary Kay Domestic Violence Foundation, Dr. Iyanla Vanzant (OWN Network) and the late, great Dr. Maya Angelou. She has been featured in media outlets including Black Enterprise Magazine; Savannah Herald; Savannah Tribune; Chicago Defender; Chicago Access Network TV, *Unveil'D* Celebrity News Magazine, and the Steve Harvey, Michael Baisden and Tom Joyner Radio Shows.

Her Professional Affiliations include: National Baptist Convention, USA, Inc.; Gullah Geechee Sea Islands Coalition; *Spirit of Excellence* Business Awards (Stellar Productions); 'Toots for Books' Literacy Foundation; Professional Woman Network; National Women Veterans United; Veterans of Foreign Wars (VFW); Frank Callen Boys and Girls Club Alumni Association and Delta Sigma Theta Sorority, Inc. Her personal accolades include Outstanding Georgia Citizen, Two (2) Guinness World Records, a BET *Her* Humanitarian Award, Reaching Back Foundation Phenomenal Woman Award, 'Keys to the City' for Eight (8) United States locales and countless other Military and Civilian Awards and Commendations.

Stacy shares her life experiences and relies on faith-based doctrines to motivate and inspire others to achieve their best mental, physical and spiritual health. She has Degrees in Education, Health Services Management, Christian Leadership and Business Administration. A Proverbs 31 Woman, she is blessed with many God-given gifts. She is the proud mother of two adult children: KeiSha and William. She and her husband, Clarence, have a beautiful blended family of five children and Grandchildren who affectionately call her 'GiGi.'. Their family is active in their church and the community. To God be the Glory!

The War at Home

My uniform's inspection-ready; ribbons and devices are in place.

Now, if only I could cover up the bruises on my face.

Maybe I'll stop at a local drugstore... but... I do not suppose,

A foundation can conceal my black eyes and broken nose.

I have fought in many battles - abuse is the agony of defeat.

Until I have an escape plan, it's a secret that I must keep.

No one will ever understand how such devastation could be so.

But my life is threatened daily, and no one can ever know.

How do I face my Shipmates or put in an honest day at work -?

When I can barely open my eyes and my body's bruised and hurt?

Maybe I'll call in sick today; just spend some time alone.

I wear the cloth of our nation but I'm fighting 'The War at Home.'

What will I tell my Superiors? How do I make them understand?

That for days on end I suffer abuse at my angry husband's hand?

My children are in danger, too, and we all need reprieve.

But he assured me he will kill us all if we ever try to leave.

Where could we go that he can't find us? Is there anywhere safe to hide?

We are in desperate need of shelter; a safe place to abide.

We are in need of help, Lord, and we need it right away!

His temper becomes more dangerous the longer that we stay.

I serve 'For God and Country' - securing others' liberty.

I even fight for my husband's freedom - yet he's abusing me!

I am praying for a breakthrough - praying the danger will soon be gone.

I wear the cloth of our nation but I'm fighting 'The War at Home.'

As I slowly opened my eyes and painfully tried to lift my head from the pillow so I could assess my surroundings, I fought back tears at the enormous heaviness of my body, as well as my spirit. Am I in a hospital? What happened? I could hear the constant sound of the machines keeping me alive. *Beep! Beep! Beep! Beep!* Standing at my bedside were doctors, nurses and a few other people I didn't recognize. Camped out in a corner of the room were both of my children, asleep on a recliner. They looked so peaceful. And even though I was in a lot of pain... I was happy to see that they were okay. Thank God!

One of the physicians, Dr. Williams, moved closer to me and said, "Good morning, Stacy. It's wonderful to see you. Welcome back. You're at Telfair Mercy Hospital. You were hurt pretty badly but you're fine now." I had a tube down my throat, so I wasn't able to speak. I wanted to ask him what happened to me. I needed to know why I was there. He kept talking but his words were muffled because I was so confused that I started to tune him out. Maybe it was the medication. Maybe it was the headache that was clouding my vision. Maybe it was the fact that I hate the smell of hospitals.

Whatever the reason, his words were lost in the air because my mind wandered and carried me to a place of euphoria. I closed my eyes and tears streamed down both sides of my face. A voice from somewhere echoed throughout every corner of mind screaming... *'I'm alive! I'm alive! God did not abandon me. I'm alive!'*

As I laid there, dazed and confused... I fought to remember what happened to me. How did I end up here... in this place? I slowly drifted into a light sleep. I silently pleaded with my mind to remember what happened because none of this made any sense to me. Eerie thoughts slowly crept into my head. I remembered hearing gun shots. *BANG! BANG! BANG! BANG! BANG!* I remembered falling to the floor. I remembered being in total darkness. I could hear glass breaking and screams echoing like thunder. But... who was screaming? Did I get shot or did I shoot someone? *Think, Stacy, think.* My body felt pain like it never had before. I couldn't breathe. I couldn't move. My memory was slowly coming back to me. I was remembering...

I laid there in silence as the doctors examined my body from head to toe. One of them asked, "Who did this to you? Miss, tell me, do you know?" I had been beaten so many times but this time I refused to tell another lie "My husband," I softly whispered while I waited there to die. Then I heard the doctors say, "A concussion to her right temple. Three fractures to her skull. There are knife wounds on her arms; she was cut with something dull. There's a burn on her right forearm, how it got there isn't clear. A black eye and a broken nose. She's bleeding from both ears. Her ribs are bruised and swollen - on the left and on the right. It's a miracle she's still alive. She was in an awful fight. She is wounded on her lower back and on her stomach, too. She has defense wounds on her hands but there was not much she could do.

It feels as though her left ankle is broken; maybe it's just a sprain. Her breathing is labored and shallow. She's in a lot of pain. A morphine drip and antibiotics will help her pain subside. She's hanging on for dear life but her unborn child has died. Then, there I was three weeks later, awakening in a daze. I was numb and I felt powerless. Everything was in a haze. I remembered what my husband did to me. My heart was broken and torn. My mind was consumed with bitterness. My heart was filled with scorn. I heard a voice say, *"You must forgive him for what he's done to you. There is purpose in your pain - a reason for all you're going through. This is another step along your journey. Your testimony is your life.*

I purposed you to be VICTORIOUS! Not a battered wife!"

Happy Birthday United States Navy

There it was. A painful reflection of what happened when Derrick and I returned from the Navy Ball that Saturday night in October. I was looking forward to a wonderful evening and the Navy Band would be great again this year, playing many old and new songs for us all to enjoy. Derrick seemed nervous about going because this would be his first time going to a Military Ball. While we were at home getting ready to go to the Ball, out of the blue he said, "Look, this isn't my thing. I'd rather we just stay at home and watch television, maybe rent some movies."

Now, he knew I was up for a Promotion and that as the Morale, Welfare and Recreation Officer at my Command, I had worked on the committee for months to make this event a success. Our ticket sales were up to 475; last year we sold 320 tickets, and everyone raved about how much better this year's Ball would be. And besides, this year I would not be going alone. I was married now, and Derrick would be with me. It would be fun, or so I thought.

When we arrived at the Hotel Del Coronado, the place was already packed. All of the Committee Members agreed to arrive at 1700 hours (5:00pm). But I spent so much time arguing with Derrick that we didn't arrive until 1815 (6:15pm). My Dinner Dress Blue Uniform Skirt was still a little wrinkled from when Derrick had crumpled it and threw it over the bedroom balcony onto the lawn while I was getting dressed.

I had just picked up my uniform from the dry cleaners earlier that morning while running errands. And simply ironing my skirt was not enough; it needed to be professionally pressed but there wasn't time. I was upset about it, but he didn't care.

He simply didn't want to go to the Ball. I suggested that we just go for the Opening Ceremony and leave before dinner was served. I even suggested that I go alone and return home in a couple of hours. He was opposed to that idea and reluctantly decided to go. Arriving over an hour late was embarrassing but I knew it would be even more embarrassing when we would get up to leave early. As we drove to the valet parking stand, Derrick turned to me and said, "Don't think that just because you'll be with your friends and colleagues that I won't put you in your place. You may be an Officer, but your uniform is not bulletproof."

He reached over and opened the glove compartment and pulled out his gun. He rubbed it along my left thigh and laughed. He then put it back in the glove compartment and closed it. He reached for my left hand and held it tightly. I sat in the car, stunned at his words and his actions. He had the nerve to do this - just before we were getting ready to get out of the car. The evening went downhill from there.

As we approached the red-carpet entrance, we ran into my Executive Officer, Captain Dobson and his wife, Victoria. Pleasant greetings and introductions were made, and Derrick and I proceeded into the ballroom.

We were late for the Social Hour and I had missed my meeting with the other Committee Members, but it was okay. I knew they were wondering where I was because a few of them had called and texted to make sure I was okay. I told them I was not feeling very well but assured them that we would be there.

Lieutenant Laura Jackson, who I share an office with, was standing near the table where the Silent Auction items were beautifully displayed. As soon as she saw us, she walked over to me and announced very loudly, "Well, well, well. Look who *finally* decided to show up. YOU were supposed to set up the Silent Auction - not ME. Thanks for your help!" Clearly, she was upset with me because before I could say a word, she walked away.

Derrick gripped my arm tightly and mentioned how embarrassed he was. *What?!* I couldn't believe it. I was the one who was yelled at, in a crowded, public venue, but HE was embarrassed. I apologized to him for the spectacle that was made. He then told me he was ready to go. I was getting annoyed at this point because we hadn't been there ten minutes and he was ready to leave. I tried to reason with him but to no avail. We left the Ballroom and walked briskly to the Valet Parking Stand and waited for the driver to bring our car around.

On the way home, the tension was overwhelming. We barely said ten words to each other. I was hungry so I opened my evening bag to nibble on the fruit snacks I had in there.

I offered Derrick some but as soon as I took them out of my bag, he snatched the bag from my hand, let the driver side window down and threw the fruit snacks and my evening bag out of the car window. I didn't say anything because I didn't want to argue. We continued the car ride in deafening silence. When we finally arrived at home, there was a strange feeling in the air. Katara and Walter, Jr. were with my best friend, Seleste, for the weekend so Derrick and I could have some quality time alone. In fact, this weekend was another phase in our marriage where we were 'starting fresh.' Our arguments had been getting worse.

His abuse was increasing, and I was three months pregnant with our first child together. He had two daughters from a previous marriage and had always wanted a son. I remember the day of our ultrasound like it was yesterday. Derrick took me to breakfast at the Rose Garden Café, one of my favorite restaurants. We talked and laughed the whole time. That was the Derrick I fell in love with six months ago. After breakfast, we went to the doctor's office. When we found out that everything was going well with the pregnancy, we were both happy. When asked by the Obstetrician if we wanted to know the sex of the baby, we looked at each other and said, "Yes" in unison.

We watched our baby on the screen and listened to a strong heartbeat for a couple of minutes. Then, there it was as plain as day: we were having a boy. When Derrick started smiling, I thought it was a moment of transformation. And it was until he turned to me and said, "Wow, Stacy. You finally did something right."

I have no idea why I thought about that morning, but it weighed heavily on me - this evening in particular. I was emotionally exhausted, and I figured it was probably hormones and followed my husband inside. The moment he closed and locked the door my life changed forever.

Six months into our perfect marriage, there I was in the hospital... again. This time was different. I didn't have the mental capacity to tell another lie about how I got my injuries. I had run out of excuses: "I fell down the stairs." "I tripped over a shoe." "I walked into a door." "I burned my hand on the stove." Enough was enough! I had told so many lies to cover up his abusive ways that I started to believe that it really was my fault. I was starting to think that if I had just gotten out of the Navy when he asked me to that things wouldn't have been so bad. He wanted to move back to North Carolina where he was from. He always complained that California was too far away from everything and everyone he knew. Being from Savannah, Georgia I was far from home also, but I had my children with me. So, it wasn't so bad.

Lying in that hospital room was a turning point in my life. I was in total disbelief because this could not possibly be happening to me. Just six shorts months ago, I had a great life, and everything was going well for me. I had two amazing children, a good job, a nice home and two luxury cars parked in my garage. And, the icing on the cake, I had married the most wonderful man imaginable.

He was the perfect man. Charming. Caring. Affectionate. Good looking. Well-known and respected in the community. Active in the church... like I said... Perfect.

Derrick and I were introduced by a mutual acquaintance of ours at a New Year's Eve Party in Temecula, California. Everyone was dressed to impress in tailored Tuxedos, beautiful evening gowns, expensive jewelry and the mansion where the party was held was magnificent. It was like a dream and I felt as though it was a fantasy of mine that I had long forgotten. Everyone in attendance was talking, laughing, dancing and having a great time - anticipating the countdown to the stroke of midnight.

Of course, with it being New Year's Eve, I did not want to bring in the new year by myself. So, when Mariah suggested that Derrick and I get to know each other, it seemed like the answer to a burning question: 'What is there to look forward to in the coming year?' Sure, I was enjoying my life. However, there seemed to be something missing. My late husband Walter had been killed in a car accident nearly five years ago and it seemed impossible to move on with my life. So, when Mariah introduced Derrick and I to each other, I knew what it was I was missing... a man.

My friend, Seleste, had told me time and time again, "Girl, you have everything in the world going for you: great kids, house, money, career - everything except a man!" Her words echoed in my head each night that I crawled into bed alone, or whenever our group of friends got together for an evening out or some social event. Seeing other couples together made me long for someone to share my life with.

Sure, I had my children, but since their father's untimely death, I had given up on ever dating again - let alone remarrying. I had decided that I would not tempt fate by starting all over again.

But tonight... there was something magic in the air and I wanted it to continue long past midnight and into the new year. I thought... maybe Seleste is right. Maybe I did need to get over Walter and move on with my life. Besides, it had been years since his death. And even though he had passed on, I still loved him.

Well... there we were. Derrick and I sitting on a bench outside under the stars. We had been talking for what seemed like hours but of course, it had been more like forty-five minutes. The connection we shared made me feel as though we had known each other forever - even though we had just met. We talked about everything under the sun: family, friends, careers, hobbies, interests. You name it - we discussed it. All I could remember is how good he made me feel just being in his presence.

As the night progressed and the midnight hour approached, Derrick and I made our way back inside to rejoin the party. He held my hand tightly, as if to say 'Yes. She's with me.' It felt good.

As the clock continued to race toward midnight, we waited with anticipation, along with the other partygoers. We all held glasses of champagne in preparation for the celebratory toast. And couples grew excited at the thought of kissing their significant others at the stroke of midnight: an age-old tradition for lovers.

Ten. Nine. Eight. Seven. Six. Five. Four. Three. Two. One. Happy New Year!!! Wow!!! Confetti everywhere, party horns being blown and there we were, Derrick and I, our lips locked in a passionate kiss - ringing in the new year. All around us we could hear the crowd singing choruses of Auld Lang Syne.

'Should auld acquaintance be forgot and never brought to mind?
Should auld acquaintance be forgot and days of auld lang syne?
For auld lang syne, my dear, for auld lang syne.
We'll tak a cup o' kindness yet for days of auld lang syne.'

Derrick and I did not even bother to stop kissing and join in the singing. We just stood there in an endless lip lock. At some point, Seleste approached and tapped my shoulder, signaling that everyone was staring at us. The music had stopped, the toast had been made and everyone was covered in confetti. Derrick and I looked at each other and laughed until we cried happy tears. Something magical and mystical happened and we were lucky enough to start off the new year together.

Love is in the Air!

It was early one Wednesday morning in January when Derrick proposed. I stood inside my living room watching from a window to see Katara and Walter Jr. get on the school bus. San Diego has the most beautiful mornings and I looked forward to finally getting Orders there. I was thirty-seven and much too young to be a widow.

Things were going well with Derrick and I was excited about having him meet Katara and Walter, Jr. someday soon. We had only been dating a few weeks and it was much too soon for them to meet him. Once the kids boarded their bus and headed to school, I grabbed my briefcase from the table in the foyer, walked out the door and locked it. I turned around and proceeded down my front porch steps and to my surprise - there was Derrick - standing in my front yard carrying a giant bouquet of long-stemmed Peach roses. It was as if he appeared out of nowhere, right then and there, he proposed to me. Caught up in the moment, I said, "Yes." We shared a lingering embrace and a kiss that seemed to go on forever. Just like on New Year's Eve.

We spoke briefly and went separate ways because I had to get to work for an important meeting. He flew into San Diego for a convention and would only be visiting from Raleigh, North Carolina for a few days. As I was driving to the 32nd Street Naval Base, it occurred to me that I didn't remember telling Derrick where I lived. Then, I thought maybe Mariah gave him my address so he could surprise me. Anyway, what did it matter? He was in town and we would certainly spend time together.

That day at work was chaotic and meetings were filled with tough decisions that were crucial for the success of our impending deployment. As tensions were rising in the Middle East, and in other places around the world, it was inevitable that more Troops would be sent overseas during this time of unrest.

All I could think about was how to make this all work with Derrick. Seleste was my best friend and I knew I could count on her to take care of Katara and Walter, Jr. during my extended absences and Deployments. But what about Derrick? Our long-distance relationship was still fresh and new. And today he proposed, and I was still processing the thought of remarrying - especially a man I barely knew. Was I overthinking this? Was I ready for such a huge change in my life?

While I sat there in the meeting, I heard a loud noise that snapped me back to reality. Commander Jacobson banged his fist on the table while declaring, "Pack your bags, Shipmates, we're going on deployment in two weeks." I was horrified. *Two weeks?* But I just got engaged! As soon as the meeting was adjourned, I texted Derrick and told him to meet me for lunch.

We met at an outdoor Café about ten minutes from the base. I explained to him that we were deploying in two weeks. He seemed aloof and said, "No, they're deploying in two weeks. You're not going. Can't you tell them that you're getting married and that you want out of your military contract?

As an Officer, you can resign your Commission, right?" "Derrick," I said, "I'm not resigning. It's taken me sixteen years to reach this point in my Naval career. Ten years as an Enlisted Sailor and six years as an Officer. There's no way I'm quitting now. Besides, I can retire in a few years." "Look," he said, "I'm not waiting until after you return from a deployment to get married. I'm not waiting until you retire.

We can go to the Court House and get married before you leave." It sounded like a good idea to me, but it all seemed very sudden. Derrick and I decided to wait until I returned from my brief ninety-day deployment. He met Katara and Walter, Jr. two days before the small ceremony. The night that I introduced him to my children, Katara told me that she got a 'weird' vibe from Derrick. She said, "Mom, I can't believe you're gonna marry him." I told her, "You're not old enough to make those decisions for me. Don't you want me to be happy?" She nodded her head 'Yes' and went to her room. I couldn't believe she was raining on my parade. *How dare she!*

Here Comes the Bride

A week later at a Court House in San Diego Derrick and I were married. Mariah and her husband, John, were witnesses. No other guests, nor any of our children were at the ceremony. Derrick thought it was best that since his children *couldn't* attend, then my children *shouldn't* attend. It made perfect sense. Besides, there was plenty of time for all of us to get together.

Happy Honeymoon?

After our small Court House wedding, Derrick and I flew to Destin, Florida for our honeymoon. Seleste was taking care of Katara and Walter, Jr. and she would also house sit for me until we returned.

Of course, she lectured me, again, about moving *way* to
Derrick *and* rushing into a marriage with a man I barely k
reminded me to be careful and to call her if I needed to. *Really?* I
was going on my Honeymoon. Why would I need to call *her* or
anyone else for that matter?

Derrick and I arrived in Destin in style. He hired a limousine
to pick us up from the airport and drive us around the city.
Everything was beautiful this time of year. I was glad that he suggested
we get married in April because there was just something special
about Spring Weddings. We arrived at our two-bedroom Villa on the
outskirts of town, right on the coast. It was breathtakingly beautiful.
The ocean breeze was inviting. Just the right amount of sun shone
through the windows.

The home was decorated in a quaint, nautical theme with
extra amenities. The Master Suite had an oversized, California King
size bed with a jacuzzi bathtub in the center of the room that could
easily fit ten people. The Chef's Kitchen was enormous, and the
dining room boasted a table and chair setting for twelve. The living
room had an old-world feel, as if it were designed several centuries
ago and preserved for our Wedding day. The color palette was of
several shades of blue with small hints of peach. Being from Georgia,
Derrick surprised me with a little 'hint of home,' as he called it.

We were both tired from such a long day and by this time we
were hungry. We didn't have a reception after our wedding because
Derrick said he was anticipating our Honeymoon.

Besides, we ate a small meal on the plane, but that was not enough to sustain us. We ordered room service and listened to music and talked while we waited for our meals.

Roughly half an hour later, we enjoyed our meal of lobster, king and Dungeness crab, grilled chicken breasts, steamed vegetables, wild rice, clam chowder, Key lime pie and cheesecake. We enjoy a beautiful, romantic dinner. Afterwards, we went for a stroll on the beach so we could watch the sunset on the horizon while we walked along the shore. It was magical.

As night slowly moved in and the stars danced for us in the Florida sky, Derrick and I returned to our Villa. We decided to settle in for our Honeymoon Night. I went to get the lingerie I had purchased for tonight from my suitcase. As I walked toward the closet, I felt a sharp pain in the center of my back. I turned to see what had hit me and Derrick slapped me so hard across the face that I stumbled backward and nearly fell into the glass coffee table in the living room. I was startled and tried to get away from him, but he was like a tiger - pouncing on its prey. I opened my mouth to scream but the sound got stuck in my throat. This was a nightmare! Derrick grabbed me by my hair and told me that if I made a sound, he would kill me. I was mortified!

The rage in his eyes was unbelievable. He slapped, kicked, and punched me - tossing me around the room like a rag doll. I felt helpless and didn't try to fight back because I didn't want to make him even more angry. What had I done? What made him treat me this way? This man beat me on our Wedding Night!!!

Finding Peace Among Broken Pieces

I woke up the following morning with the sun beaming upon my face. I was in immense pain, but I was also numb at the same time. I couldn't believe that Derrick, my loving and wonderful husband did this to me. Why?

I was supposed to be happy but instead there I lay in a beautiful villa on the beach. The morning after my wedding. On my honeymoon. And, the night before, instead of becoming a blushing bride... I had become a battered wife.

I spent my days and nights from that day forward living in fear. I lied and made excuses for Derrick. I was too ashamed to tell anyone what was happening to me. When he decided to leave Raleigh and join me, Katara and Walter, Jr. in San Diego, I turned my attention to keeping my children safe. I never left them alone with him and I always kept emergency cash hidden away - just in case. I got my legal affairs in order and made sure that Seleste had my sister, Lymond's, telephone number. She would need to know who to call if Derrick ever made good on his promise to kill me.

He was vicious to me in private but the perfect, loving husband to me in public. He was like a Jekyll and Hyde; two different people, sharing one body. Did I take his threats of death seriously? Absolutely! I believed him when he said he loved me. I also believed him when he said he would kill me.

I wanted to leave. I needed to leave but I had to get away with my life and the lives of my children. Each time Derrick beat me, he would later bring me flowers, sometimes candy, too. He always promised to do better 'this time.' Somehow convincing me that he would change. He would blame his temper on his job, his difficulty adjusting to California or me. He would blame me!

Another Step Along My Journey

Knock. Knock. Knock. The faint sound of knocking caused me to slowly awaken again. How long was I asleep? The hospital staff had all left the room. Katara and Walter, Jr. were also gone. I was alone. Dr. Williams entered my room, along with two Police Officers. I laid there and listened to one of them, read me my Miranda Rights. I was being placed under arrest for the assault and battery of one, Derrick Broussard! It took nearly eight months for all of the evidence to be gathered, sorted out and analyzed. By the Grace of God, the charges against me were dropped and the case was dismissed.

As for Derrick, he sustained minor injuries on that October night, but he was eventually arrested, indicted and found guilty of numerous felony charges and sentenced to seventeen years in prison. With him behind bars I was able to start rebuilding my life.
He wrote me several letters, pleading for another 'fresh start' promising that he would 'do better.' I had heard those words too many times before.

This time, I would not believe his lies. There was no chance for reconciliation. I filed for, and was granted, a Divorce which he did not contest. He knew it was over for good this time. We both knew. As for me, I am still healing and starting to feel better about myself. Each day, little by little, my wounds heal, my mind is refreshed, and my spirit is renewed.

Stacy L. Henderson, the woman behind the uniform, is on the road to recovery. This new journey is taking me 'From Pain to Purpose.' My children are healing as well, as a result of the abuse they witnessed. One day at a time. One day at a time... hope and love is being restored. Thank God!

Donna Marie Lambert

FB: Donna.m.lambert

IG: dmaries_beauty_for_you

Donna M. Lambert is a licensed Cosmetologist for 30 plus years. She has owned and managed her styling salon for five years. She has supervised salons for corporate salons for three years. She has been very influential in advising aspiring hair stylists to complete their training to become certified and licensed. She has trained and coached stylists to excel in their craft. She has knowledge of business and professionalism by working with corporations and non-profit organizations. She is also a Beauty Consultant and has been trained by Fashion Fair, Ultima 2, Avon and Mary Kay Cosmetics. She is now a Paparazzi Independent Consultant Director selling affordable fashion jewelry and leading a team.

Ms. Donna has been a Superintendent of Sunday Schools for the Apostolic Church Ministries in Mount Vernon, New York. She is a licensed minister and an ordained Pastor. She currently conventionally teaches women of different cultures life application according to the Scriptures. Her students today are American, African and Caucasian Women and children. She is an advocate of Domestic and sexual abuse.

Most of her work is done behind her chair in the salon, as she lends a listening ear and support to those that she comes in contact with. She has inspired others by sharing bits and pieces of her story to take their power back and walk in victory.

Degree: Associate of Applied Science Culinary Arts

Certification: ● Certified Professional Diversity Trainer-Women's Issues

Other Certifications:

● JCP Train the Trainer

● Chef training

● Serv Safe

● Domestic Violence 101

CRY OUT, GET OUT, STAY OUT

When I first experienced domestic violence, I was about nine years old. My issues of fear stem from this traumatic experience. I felt paralyzed, which caused me to live in silence half of my life. What I want to share with you through my story is the importance of crying out, getting out and staying out of all domestic violence relationships. Let me share a little background of who I am. Growing up, I was the oldest of seven siblings. I am an offspring of statutory rape. My mother was sixteen years old and my father was twenty when he had sex with her. Back in the day, you were arrested for behavior like that. Likely so, my grandfather, my mother's father, had him arrested. I believe this set the stage for my life's journey of sexual and domestic violence. My father was released from prison after doing his time and for the second time he impregnated my mom. Before baby number two came the two of them got married. Although they never divorced, their marriage didn't last very long. The man I remember most of my younger years was my mother's male friend, whom I called daddy.

My daddy was a little younger than my mother, and my mom was only seventeen years older than I was. With that being said, my daddy decided to have his cake and ice cream all at the same time. That is how we usually like to eat cake with ice cream, right? I don't want to make my story about my mother, but she was indirectly involved in my experiences. My mother was a battered woman. I hated to hear her cry through their bedroom door. It broke my heart to hear her cry.

My mom was a stay at home mom up until I was nine years old. My daddy would leave to go to work about noon five days a week. Before my mom actually started her job, I remember a meeting the three of us had in the kitchen. The two of them thought it was time that I heard the story about the birds and the bees. So, this is when I was told about my menstruation cycle, that's all I remember. My mom would now leave to travel to work very early in the morning on the New York City subway system.

Being the oldest, I helped get my siblings get dressed and ready for the day. Soon as they were ready my daddy would send them outside to play in the park across the street as he held me back to stay with him. I don't remember the time frame, but I know it felt like a lifetime. Have you ever, as a little girl, put tissues in your little training bra? Well, I did, and that was before the conversation about the birds and the bees. This man took it upon himself to show me how I could get my breasts to grow without tissues. He performed sexual acts on my breast, and he told me "don't think about telling mom" because he did the same thing to her. He made it seem like this was a normal thing to do.

To this day, I don't remember everything but what I do remember is too much. I subconsciously have blocked out some incidents. I cannot tell you how many times this happened, but I know for sure it was a continual occurrence. The other time that comes to mind, which I've never forgotten, is when he took me to their bedroom and made me take all my clothes off. He then did the same thing.

I felt so ashamed and afraid that someone was going to see us. The windows at that time were wide open, blinds and curtains too. This was the big set up. He did everything sexually to me but insert his penis into me. He guided me on what to do to him sexually as well. This all took place while my mom was at work and my siblings were at the park.

During this time, it seemed like I didn't hear my mom cry as much, I don't know, maybe it was all in my little nine-year-old imagination. I became very angry and very protective of my siblings, especially my brother. One day I took up for my brother and my daddy took both his hands and sandwich smacked my face. This was the beginning of the physical abuse, the beating, smacking and oh boy that big black leather belt was no joke on my naked behind. Yes, he would always make me take all my clothes off when he was ready to beat me.

The abuse ended from him when he slammed my mom's head on a hot boiler. My mom had a burn on her forehead the size of a softball. I saw him do that to her. I felt so bad for my mom. This was one beating that she couldn't hide from her brothers. This ended the cycle of abuse in her life and it was the end to a beginning of sexual and physical abuse for me. Innocent Donna was gone! I spent my teenage years looking for someone to complete the job that he had started. The boys in the Bronx that I liked were always older than me. They would kiss me, but they would not touch me sexually. I'm very happy about that now, but then I didn't understand why they didn't want to do to me what my daddy had done to me.

I carried that secret with me for many years. I didn't cry out. I was threatened not to tell my mom or else. Or else what? I don't know!

What I do know is that he was very mean to my mom, my brother and I, so I wasn't going to go against what he ordered me not to do. Four of us were from my father and mother's marriage and my three younger siblings belonged to my daddy. My daddy was a factory worker and he would bring home cut out stretch pants. He would show me how to sew them together. That was the only good I saw in him other than giving me three beautiful young sisters.

My sperm donor father came to live with us for a short while. He was abusive in other ways. I don't remember much about him being financially there for us. What I know of my father is, in his presence, he was very absent. I'm grateful that he never put his hands on me in any way.

At this time, in the early 70's, the Bronx was being condemned and we had to relocate. We moved to Mount Vernon, New York, which was in the next county north of the city. I was alright with the move somewhat until I had to leave my high school and transfer to Mount Vernon High School. I was fifteen years old, in the last half of my tenth-grade year, feeling like my world had crumbled. I met this boy in high school, and it was with him that I gave away my virginity, well what was left of it. It was the worst feeling and I hated having sex with him. There were no good feelings in it for me at all. This continued for about a year. I got my first job at McDonald's and it was there that I met my husband.

He claimed me as his wife, and I fell for the flattery. We im
started to date. We went out dining, partying and we would
hustle dance and win dance contests. While we were seventeen, he
asked my Mom for my hand in marriage. My mother said yes but she
did not mean yes. She saw something in him that I was too blind to
see. I was head over heels in love with him. He and I began to plan
our wedding, which would be September 4, 1976.

During our engagement, we still liked to party and one night
we went to a house party. Together, we went downstairs to the
basement where the party was being held at. He decided to leave me
there. I was extremely uncomfortable down there with people I did
not know. Furthermore, I didn't come to the party with him to sit
down there without him. I came upstairs to the outside looking for
him. He was being his charming self, in the middle of a crowd of
young women like myself.

I expressed my desire to leave the party and so I proceeded to
walk out of the backyard to the sidewalk to walk home. He rushed
over to me telling me to stay and I said that I was ready to leave and I
was leaving. At that time, he got mad at my decision to leave the party
and he punched me in my face and to the ground I went. His best
friend grabbed him off of me and said "man, what are you doing?"
So, I ran away as fast as I could. I took off my engagement rings and
threw them as far as I could throw them.

When he caught up with me, I told him that I wasn't going to marry him. Well, he purchased another set of rings and convinced me that he would never do anything like that again. If someone is reading this and has been through similar situations, you know that that was only the beginning of a vicious cycle of abuse. If you are in an abusive relationship now and you are reading this just know that it's probably a lie. I had all the signs that I was about to do the wrong thing by walking down that aisle.

I received a phone call from a friend, whom I still to this day call my BFF. He said, "You're really going to go through with this?" While I was on the call, two hours late for the wedding, I received a dozen red roses from my soon to be husband. I didn't want to go through with it, but I didn't know how not to at the time. Even when I was about to march down the aisle to the song, Here Comes the Bride, I was stepping backwards. My uncle, who was giving me away, said "baby girl you do not have to go through with this!" I did it anyway, and it was the saddest day of my life.

We had plans to take the money we had received as gifts and go to Atlantic City in New Jersey for our honeymoon. Instead, he wanted to stay back, spend the money on weed, get high and have a lot of sex. All the time my family thought I was away on my honeymoon. The isolation started then. I didn't call my Mom or my siblings, it was just him, his mother and me. His Mother knew we hadn't gone anywhere.

After the honeymoon was over my husband had enlisted to go into the military. When the officers came to pick him up to go, he decided not to answer the door. I was already enrolled in college and I attended until I began to fall asleep in class every day. It was at this time that I realized I was pregnant. As a result of my pregnancy, I decided to drop out of college at that time.

My husband wasn't working, and he began to live the street life, always fighting and getting into trouble. My husband got into a fight and he defended himself by a breaking a glass bottle and digging it into a young man's face. As a result of his actions, a group of guys came after him and gave him the beating that he didn't see coming. His mother decided to send him off to Florida.

When I finally joined him there, he already had a girlfriend, which made me sad, hurt, hopeless and pretty angry. I went on being his little housewife while he cheated on me. He demanded that I cut up his meat in bite size pieces like he was a child. He would call me names, and if I didn't want to have sex, he would force me to. I hated the things he wanted me to do sexually to him and when I refused one time, he slammed my hand behind the headboard. I guess he figured I didn't need hands if they weren't going to be catering to his sexual desires. The next incident, he decided to bring his girlfriend to our apartment, and I was furious. I was so mad that I wouldn't stop yelling at him to get her out of there.

He was frustrated because I wouldn't keep quiet, so he punched me, and I landed on my back on the floor, six months pregnant mind you. The cheating continued and the abuse escalated to the point that I finally called my mother to come help me. My mom came down on the Greyhound bus to get me. My husband demanded that I go to the hospital before I travel on a bus for twenty-four hours. He knew without a shadow of a doubt that the doctor would tell me I'm too close to my delivery date to travel on a bus 24 or more hours. It must have been the grace and mercy of the Most High, my Power, that told the doctor to tell me that it was probably a good thing for me to travel. The doctor said after that long ride I would be ready to give birth when I got back home to Mount Vernon. The Most High knew best and delivered me out of there. I was due on the 14th of June 1977 and left Florida on the 12th. I had a beautiful healthy baby girl on June 16, 1977. I cried out, and got out, but I did not stay out!

The summer of 1977 my mom decided to move to Maryland, which is where one of her brothers had been living for years. She had said if she ever got the opportunity to leave New York that she would and would never come back. My mom, her mom, my siblings, my baby girl and I relocated to live in Maryland. My grandmother and I shared an apartment, and my mom was in the same building with my siblings. Although I wasn't divorced or legally separated yet, I began to date a guy that lived in the building that we lived at.

My grandmother, being old fashioned, laid down the house rules and told me that I couldn't have another man in this house but my husband. I only communicated with my husband sometimes. Shortly after the conversation with my grandmother, my husband and I decided to get back together. My husband moved to Maryland with us. He seemed to find his way around Maryland pretty good. He was very involved in drugs, not only using them but now he was selling them as well. He told me that if I didn't join in with him that he would find a woman that would. He showed me how to use several different illegal drugs. It was at this time he also taught me how to be a drug dealer. He showed me how to weigh, pack and sell the products.

My daughter was now about eighteen months old. She saw an album cover with something on it and she picked it up to play with it. All this man's weed fell to the floor that had green shag carpet on it. I couldn't decipher the weed from the green shag carpet, I tried so hard to find it. My poor baby girl got the spanking of her life from her father. This caused a lot of interference with my family. One of my five sisters was at my apartment visiting her 1st born niece, our daughter, at the time. My husband and my sister began to exchange words about the spanking, and it was then that my sister left and went down the hall to the apartment that my family lived in. My grandmother came out of her bedroom to see what all the commotion was about. My husband reacted by getting his gun out of the safe and proceeded to aim the gun toward my grandmother and my siblings in the hallway.

The situation got very ugly when my husband kicked the sister that had just left the apartment in her forehead. We were all fighting trying to get him away from my family.

Now, I am on baby number two and the abuse is escalating once again. This man found any excuse to abuse me. He got angry at me for anything. For example, he told me my strides was too short. He demanded that I take longer steps when I walk. I don't know what I did or didn't do right this time, but he decided to remove a closet door from the hinges and began to beat me with it. He went from beating me with the door to dragging me to our balcony to throw me off of it. My heavenly Father spared my life and he didn't throw me over. We lived on the third or fourth floor in a high-rise building.

I was so unhappy, and I just couldn't for the life of me understand why this man thought it was alright to continue to beat me. I was always focused on doing things the way he wanted me to, thinking that crossing every I and dotting every T would stop him from abusing me. I always thought to myself that I was not good enough for him. I seemed to always make him mad and I blamed myself for every time he put his hands on me. Every name he called me must have been true. After all my daddy abused first, so it must be my fault.

My grandmother was going to be moving to another apartment building and it was then that we decided to move back to Mount Vernon, New York. When I got back to Mount Vernon, my mother-in-law thought it would be a good idea for me to go to beauty culture school.

As I waited to go to beauty culture school, I took a home health aide class so I would be capable of taking care of my husband's grandmother. I was happy to help out and because of the training I qualified to get paid for the job. My husband was feeling a sense of powerlessness and said to me "there's more ways to skin a cat." By him purposely getting me pregnant he felt in control again.

I couldn't understand after getting me pregnant why he would throw me down to the floor and stomp me over and over again in my stomach. My due date was near, within two weeks. He practically stomped our baby out of my stomach.

The next day I brought up everything I had eaten and from three openings on my body fluids started to leave my body including this large white lump of something. The next day I had to be taken to the hospital to deliver our baby. I was so happy that our baby boy came out healthy and full term. The idea of me attending school must have made him afraid that I would leave him again.

Time drew near for me to go to school when my baby was about eight months old. I finished school in ten months and got my license shortly thereafter in 1984. I found a job that was going to help me truly figure out how and when I was going to escape this marriage. I was working in a barbershop/Salon. When I would come home, he would accuse me of sleeping around on him with the barbers where I worked.

One evening I got home from work and my husband accused me of having sex with one of the barbers, so in the hallway right between my front door and the living room he ripped my clothes off of me and raped me right there. He said that he would be able to tell if I had been with someone sexually. After violently having sex with me, he got up off of me and said yeah you had sex with someone. I was hysterical and couldn't understand how he came up with those results. I had been faithful while we were together. My husband was not finished abusing me yet. Shortly after this incident, he beat me to the front porch, down the stairs, up the block and back down the block. In addition to the beating, what also hurt me was that his mother, her husband and the next-door neighbor sat there on the porch watching the whole thing and never helped me.

His mother later suggested that I go file papers for an order of protection. Before returning home someone that knew my husband called his mother and they told her about the papers that I had filed against her son. There were spiral steps in the back hallway, and he sent me spiraling down those steps, that's how mad he was at me. What was he so angry about and why did I choose to be the one to continue to take all those beatings?

The final incident was the most terrifying for me. He decided to get a kitchen knife and place it to my throat; I was so scared, scared out of my mind. I saw my life flash in front of me. I think he scared himself because he put the knife down and stormed out of the apartment door.

At this time, shaking like a leaf, I went to the kitchen drawer where all the knives were and put them underneath my mattress. I then sat on top of the mattress on all the knives trembling and crying. My husband's best friend, my bodyguard, just happened to call the house and I was crying hysterically. I told him what had happened, and he came to put me up in a motel in the Bronx.

I finally cried out and got out of this relationship in 1985. I left my job without notice. At that time, I didn't know myself at all. Mentally I felt unstable. Emotionally I was drained. Physically I felt like a bus ran over me. Everything got harder though because now I had so much to do. I had three beautiful children to love and take care of. I had to ask for help at social services because I had nothing. I didn't drive yet so I walked everywhere I needed to go.

I walked through Mount Vernon full of fear. I was so afraid he would see me. While walking I would duck behind cars and I would often be looking over my shoulders. All I cared about was finding a way not to go back. I was so relieved to have gotten out alive. I had to figure out where I was going to live, how I was going to take care of my three children. It was suggested that I go to a shelter for battered women. It sounded like the perfect thing to do until I was told that they didn't accept children in the program.

In a confused state, I walked up, what we called the Avenue, with a transportation coin in my hand to go to the shelter. I didn't even have a change of underwear. As I walked up the avenue, I ran into one of my co-workers, and she wanted to know why she hadn't seen me.

I told her what I was going through, and she opened up her home to my children and me. She had three children, a niece and her significant other. I ended up going to stay with her. I needed to get a job, so I went to the salon where my co-worker was now working, and I rented a booth there. This was the beginning of my career on my own. After a year I saved enough money to get my own apartment. My girlfriend didn't allow me to pay any bills while we stayed with her and her family. She gave me a cash box and told me to put all my money in there. I think I only had to buy food. I moved out into a brand-new apartment building where there were only dwellings for six families.

I was told to go to AA, Alcoholic Anonymous, and I went because I needed anything that would help me get over what I had been through. Going to AA and NA meetings helped me to get a hold of my life. I also took my children to meetings. We went through our steps and this would make my life peaceful. My children were 8, 6 and 2 ½ years old when I left my husband. I was able to forgive my husband for all the trauma and abuse he caused me; I would even invite him to our children's birthday parties.

After one of the birthday parties he pushed me up to the wall to kiss me and I did not let him. A few days later he came to my apartment door. I opened the door and he pulled out his gun on me. I yelled and screamed, and he left like a bat out of hell. I still had my order of protection. It never kept him away from me though. I opened a hair salon in 1990 and this would make my ex furious.

He told me that Mount Vernon was his town. I didn't argue with him. I didn't say a word and that made him mad. On his way out of my salon he knocked over all my supply trays, trying to destroy what I had built.

At the age of twenty-seven, not only was I going to meetings, I started therapy with a psychologist. I have to say that although I wasn't drinking or drugging anymore, something still wasn't right with me. Over the years the very people that called themselves helping me were the very same folks abusing me in disguise. During this time, I would continue to attract the same abusive men into my life. Before my first marriage was legally over my husband sent long stemmed red roses to my job. What he wrote on the card was the joke of all times to me. It read; nine years wasn't enough. I was laughing and angry all at the same time and took those roses and broke them in half and threw them in the trash can. He tricked me once, then twice but not a third. It was a wrap!

I married again to a guy that I met in the program. He was so fine, just like my first husband. He was eight years younger than me and I was flattered that he even looked at me. I thought that it was a big deal, that lets you know where my self-esteem and self-worth were. I can't say that I knew what self-esteem was. This marriage lasted a short three years. The bottom line is that I couldn't sleep at night because I was afraid that he would rape my daughter. During this three-year period, he cheated on me and gave me an STD, so we were advised by the doctor not to have sex for seven days.

He did not want to hear that, so he got very angry and insisted that I have sex with him. When I refused to have sex with him, he lifted me up and threw me to one corner of our bedroom, then to the next corner and the same to the third corner in our bedroom. I thought a cyclone had entered my bedroom and I did not know who this man was. The last throw was toward the foot of the bed. I went flying into the closet door which was directly in front of our bed and my head hit the door and my neck snapped.

After it was all over, I just crawled back in the bed trembling in pain, and all I could do was sob at what had just taken place. Now I began to wonder how and when I was going to get out of this mess, I had gotten myself into. My children were in the other two rooms, they said they thought we were just playing around. I woke up in the morning, after my husband left to go to work, then I called my therapist and she asked me if I had had enough yet? My quick reply was yes. She came to the house and took me to the emergency room. I was treated as a patient that was in an automobile accident. I left there with a neck brace on. I had him arrested, and they took him right to prison. He had the nerve to call me from prison to ask me to bail him out. Bailing him out was not going to happen by me. I had had enough. This was marriage number two down the drain.

Over the course of the twenty years I realized that I didn't know what love was, I was in search of love. I have been in three homosexual relationships looking for love and I had sex with numerous amounts of men looking for love. Yes, I had a lot of one-night stands.

My father, nor my daddy showed me what love was, so in search of it I ended up with so much baggage. How could I attract to myself what I didn't know? I kept attracting what my father and daddy showed me about love. I found abuse in several of the men that I encountered. This caused me to be very depressed. I often thought about suicide. I cried inside all the time and my heart ached daily. My eyes were the windows of my soul. People that knew me, knew when I said I was fine that I wasn't. I just couldn't hide it; my eyes told the real story. The pain and shame were very real.

My third marriage was to a man I met in church. I just knew he was the one for me. When I met him, I was in my fifth year of celibacy. I was feeling pretty good about myself. I was finally introduced to my self-esteem and my self-worth. When I shared this with him about my celibacy, he said that I wore it like a badge of honor. We carried on like we were a couple, but he would continue to tell me that I wasn't his type. He called me the funny looking lady and he said that I had a big head. He really hurt my feelings.

We were in this ministry, and the pastor told him that he had to marry me or remove himself from my life because it looked like we were a couple. The pastor expressed to him that it wasn't fair for him to be around me, getting all those benefits and not marry me. He didn't want to lose me, so he married me in May of 2001. The marriage became very controlling and abusive. He monitored the time that I spent with my friends and how late I worked. I became so depressed and gained about fifty pounds. I couldn't understand how I kept attracting the same abusive men in my life.

He punched me, kicked me, knocked me down and finally he lifted me up off the floor with his hands around my neck. He was about to take his knee and knee me in my chin while I was still up off the floor with his hands around my neck. He didn't do it. He finally let me down and I knew I was done!

In 2006, I finally had enough of the abuse. I didn't know how I was going to get out. I began to unpack and pack boxes. Whatever items were mine I put in boxes with my initial on it and all his items went in a box that had his initial on the boxes. I did this over the course of one year. One of my uncles died in April 2007, and it was the first time all my siblings had been back in New York. It was my time to escape. He told me many times to leave and go with my family. This was my opportunity. I rented a U-Haul truck, my family rolled up in eight cars and they moved me out. I have not turned back.

I finally cried out, got out and stayed out. I made a conscious decision to get to know myself in 2010. I was frightened because at fifty I had never lived alone. There were always siblings, husbands, children, or family. This was the first for me living alone. Three years passed by and I was feeling pretty good about myself. I had successfully supervised a corporate styling salon for three years. I was in college working toward my degree in culinary arts. In addition to this, I took a training in Kentucky on diversity and women's issues. I received my certification from that training. I could always tell you what I didn't like but not what I liked. I began the process, and throughout this time I started to travel.

From this point, I focused on the things I've always thought of doing and completing. I went back to college to complete my program in Culinary arts and received my Associates of Applied Science degree. Recently, I took a course on domestic violence and completed the class. I love to cook, bake, crochet and walking is my most favorite exercise. I love going on cruises, going on spiritual retreats and Disney World for family vacations. I continue to engage in domestic violence support groups.

The groups help myself and others. They help me to remember the red flags. Most of all, it helps me to remember that none of the abuse was my fault, and that I didn't deserve to be abused. One of my mastermind coaches told me to ask myself a question. The question was, was my ego more important than the help that would be received through my story? My answer was finally NO to my ego and yes to help!

Although I still feel the pain, and the tears still roll down my face sometimes, I give all praises to my Heavenly Father, that I still am a work in progress. I have been abstinent on purpose since 2010 and I am open to true love. Love doesn't hurt. I walk in victory every day that I decide to love myself and to become the person that I was created to be. I work daily on becoming the best version of myself. My prayer is that you would CRY OUT, GET OUT, and STAY OUT! You are worthy of true love and affection.

Madelaine Murphy

Waykt. Hello, in one of my languages. I am a mix of Shuswap, Okanagan, Sioux, Swedish, and Scottish. The first five years of my life I spent on my mom's reserve until the Chief and council (at the time) voted to have white men removed from the reserve, although my father is half Sioux. I had six siblings. Three are still alive today, along with me and my father. I made a promise to my grandparents and whomever could hear me that day when I was around four or five that I would never raise my children that way. I was raised in a strict, violent, and abusive home.

Our mom and my dad tried raising us kids the best they could with the knowledge and wisdom they were each taught. Unfortunately, my mom went to residential school and my dad was ripped from his mom and sisters as a baby and adopted out into a family who wanted a work horse not a child to raise. My earliest memory is of my oldest brother singing to me when I was a newborn, you are my sunshine. I sang it to each of my five children and now my granddaughter.

I remember almost always yelling and screaming, cleaning up my mom's blood, cleaning up broken pieces of whatever it was that time that got broken, watching my dad beat my brothers, setting my brothers up to fight, walking on eggshells, wondering what might set off my dad again. My mom could be mean also just in a different way. She would make fun of me, ignore me, let me know I was always in the way, tell me to go play outside with my sexual abusers.

Mom was quieter and deliberate. I remember the first time I got backhanded from my dad. I was standing up for my brother telling my dad "No, he's had enough." I remember trying to take the blame for anything and everything just to have peace. I always had a connection to Creator that would scare my mom and dad, "where did she come up with that?"

We moved to Salmon Arm when I was in grade three. The beatings slowed down. I do not remember my mom being hit or thrown around anymore. There was still emotional, mental, and some spiritual abuse within our home. I felt like an outcast in the public schools. Poor, not allowed to play afterschool, and my skin was different, so I was made fun of. I ran away from home three or four times, each time returning home. The final time my mom told me not to come back. I listened and never returned. Our neighbors brought me to my hometown, Enderby BC Canada, where I knew our reserve had its own child welfare system. I was put into care at age twelve, experiencing three homes.

The last home I was approached sexually by an older foster brother. When I tried to tell my worker, I was made out to be a liar and made to sign myself out of care at fourteen. From there I lived on the streets. I would shower when I could, usually at my friends' houses when I could spend the night or weekend. I remember being in -28° with windchill, behind the Christian Academy, between two rubber mats. I would eat where and when allowed, sometimes from grocery stores or a restaurant garbage.

I met my older two children's father after I had just turned fifteen. He was the nicest, gentlest man I had met up to that point. He lived with his mom and brothers, sometimes cousins. It was known as a party house, anything goes, no holds barred. We were together off and on until he passed away when I was 22. I never realized until years later I was mentally, emotionally, and spiritually abused and even a few times also physically abused in that relationship. I never thought about it as it was not as bad as home life.

I was 20 when I met a man close to my age and wound up pregnant with my middle child. It was at that time that I found out that my first love had acute leukemia. He had to receive treatment in Vancouver, BC. I went to visit him there with my stomach showing. I told him I made a mistake, and he said "No, a baby is a gift not a mistake." A couple months before my third was born, the biological dad came to talk to my first love, who was in remission back home. I was uneasy, to say the least. Bio dad told my first love he didn't expect to be a father anytime soon, and not with me He knew how much I loved my first love and asked if he would take care of the baby like his own? He said yes, he would. Shortly after giving birth, my first love found out the cancer was back. He passed away in Vancouver.

Alone, twenty-one and with three children, I was so upset at Creator and my first love. My children were removed from me "temporarily" the rest of their childhood lives due to neglect. Being 21 with three children, I couldn't possibly parent them properly.

I feel as if it was political, whomever is in highest power or knows someone in power, or a family member, whatever they say is taken for golden truth, even if facts are not looked at. If your own people, your own bloodline, whom you were so excited to meet your whole life can treat you like that, you learn fast who to trust and who is for themselves no matter who they need to push under to get to the top. Colonialism at its finest.

For the next ten years it was phone calls nightly at 7, visits when allowed, every weekend, even shared parenting with foster parents. I wanted to die. I could not understand why the Creator would take everything I loved away from me. I was accused of drinking, even though I never really cared to drink. My brothers who came to check on me drank, but all I usually was coffee. I even had to tell them all Chief and council is calling you all undesirables and you are not allowed around me or home. Not once did the child welfare, Chief and council, or anyone for that matter, offer any services regarding how to fix their concerns.

Having nothing to live for in my life I let alcohol and a very abusive man into my life. I had no idea he had been watching me for years. I knew this man was violent and eventually hoped he would kill me. I put up with six years of abuse that I had only ever read about but never witnessed or experienced before.

I have been held against my will, choked until I passed out numerous times, three ribs were broken and unfixable, both middle fingers were twisted from him trying to rip them off, had a broken nose I had to reset, along with an inch scar inside my mouth I cleaned up with peroxide, as I was not allowed to see a doctor for help. I have burn scars, knife scars, rug burns from being dragged, and grey hair thick where he would drag me around. I had a miscarriage from him. He choked me until I passed out. I came too, to this man raping me. I made it to the hospital, embarrassed telling them what happened. I stayed at the hospital for a few days. I knew this man was nothing but a bully and would never kill me, just torture me. I found my faith and belief in the Creator.

I knew it was time to dummy myself up before I ended up dead. I started seeing a therapist of my choice, as the one child welfare appointed me reporting to the social worker about my sessions. I needed someone I could trust. I moved to Vernon BC. I tried almost everything to break it off with my abuser, but there was no getting through. My mom and sisters moved away from my dad and were starting their lives over. I was super excited, but it was short lived. When my abuser figured out, I was trying to leave him he threatened to kill them, my kids, my dad, and other siblings if I tried leaving him. Although I felt defeated, I kept praying, talking to my ancestors, and holding my faith there would be a way out.

I became pregnant with my fourth blessing, a girl. My abuser after swearing up and down it was not his child, would keep her away from me, cutting off breastfeeding for the bottle.

I felt something was not right, as if he was grooming her like sexual predators do to their victims. I knew I had to get her out fast. I had started remembering stories of him raping women/girls intoxicated or passed out, along with the times he had raped me. I became pregnant with my last bundle of joy, a little boy. Again, was not his child, and my abuser ignored him. Throughout this time of having my last two children, I tried telling my mom and family of his plans if I left, which caused fights because I was told I was lying. By this point, I had weekend visits with my older three. Two were growing into amazing preteen women and my mind frenzied whether this abuser was also a sexual predator. I had to get away.

I went in for a tubal ligation to find out I was already pregnant with twins (I wanted twins). I explained I must have been raped again while sleeping. The doctor did an abortion before tying my tubes. I had tried having them tied before leaving the hospital with my son after birth. Unfortunately, it was against policy. I refused to register my youngest two as First Nation for fear my band would take them for being my children as my older children were removed from my care. My abuser was spending more time with his next victim, who I knew of before I left my hometown. I was hoping, praying he would stay with her and leave me alone.

My youngest sister passed away young from a car accident. Her boyfriend she was breaking up with was intoxicated from booze and cocaine. He walked away, our family drifted further apart, and harder into addictions.

I found out my sister was raped by my abuser. As my children grew, I found out he raped her in front of my kids. I don't know how many times. I absolutely lost it after her wake and funeral. I wouldn't let my abuser near my kids. I went to treatment four times, twice without children, when my children were removed, then twice with children. My youngest was about six months. I went with my two youngest, the older ones were not allowed to go with me, which made no sense as alcohol and drugs are a family disease. I knew this is how I wanted to live, free, clean, and as close to the Creator and our traditional ways.

I started when I got home. I quit drinking and started practicing our traditional way of life, living the seven teachings. I told my abuser he needed to get help, not just with drinking, but everything he had ever experienced from a child. I think he realized I was serious this time. He went to a treatment center; one I had been to before.

When I was in treatment, I would have this dream over and over, until I talked with one of the counselors there, and they suggested I ask him to go to treatment. I would wake up with the feeling of blood on me. I could smell the blood. I knew I finally got rid of him. I called the treatment center wondering if he had gotten help or even attempted to get help with raping women and girls. When they said no, I knew my dream was going to come true.

I got a phone call from the center letting me know "he exploded when asked about raping women and is on his way back to Okanagan, to be safe." I was in such panic; all I could do was pray. My sister had an appointment with a medicine man (a traditional healer and spiritual leader who serves a community of indigenous people) at Friendship Center, but he told her to come and get me right away it was important. I was shocked and puzzled, I had no idea there was a medicine man in town.

I walked in the room frightened at why he needed to see me so urgently. I had a feeling it had to do with my abuser. Hidden Wolf was gentle, funny, understanding, and wise. Within a minute I knew it was to do with my abuser and continuing my faith and belief. I told Wolf of my dream. He asked what would my kids do without both parents? I never thought about it like that. He told me hurry and get to the courthouse, get a restraining order, tell them the truth like you told me. If they don't believe you give them my name and number. Next go home and pack for a week.

I could have no contact with ANYONE I loved, he would do the rest. I received the restraining order, a thirty second response to my house, and sheriffs to serve him for safety. After we packed and were safe, I kept praying for everyone. I was frightened for my older kids, my mom and my sister.

I was so excited to see and hear everyone was safe. It took every two weeks for six months of court dates waiting to hear his side, my abuser never showed or had a lawyer present. I was given a full restraining order and full custody until he requested through courts, he was not allowed a hundred meters of me.

I was stalked for about a year from a hillside surrounding our apartment complex. I had a 2x4 fly through my bedroom window. I could feel his spirit in the area. I had to cut a lot of people out of our lives to keep us safe. Those people who were story seekers and gossipers. There were times I would feel bad his mom, sister, and brother wouldn't get to see the kids grow, and when asked if they would like to visit them, my kids would say no. As my kids grew, they said "No, we never knew them when we were little so why would we want to see them now?"

My life was getting better. I could sleep without fear of him beating me in my sleep, waking to him raping me, or just standing over me. I was seeing a therapist and alcohol drug counselor. We all agreed going to a family treatment with all my kids would be healing and allow for a fresh start. I remember telling a family support worker I had a restraining order and was told "thank goodness now you can have your children returned," strange since no one from that department said anything to me about my abuser.

We all went to treatment; this was a great learning adventure for all of us. When we got back home it was same song and dance with the child welfare program. By this time, my kids spent more than half their lives in care.

I knew my youngest girl in care loved her foster parents, and I couldn't take her security away. I quit trying for visits as she was old enough to make her own mind up to visit her mom or not. My older two learned early how to use the system. I never received my children back in my care.

The younger two and I were and are very vigilant about who knows anything about us in all parts of our lives. Unfortunately, I see post-traumatic stress syndrome in them, and myself. We joke about being able to see in the dark as we lived in the dark so no one would know we were there. We joke about making a weapon out of anything. We all know there is a boogeyman in real life, not a made-up character on TV, we lived it. I tried to shelter my kids from all the ugliness and evil I had seen or heard as a child but becoming an alcoholic I never knew the effects it would have on my children.

I never let my children see me beat up, until I had my youngest two. I would make myself better before the visit. I knew they all heard us yelling and fighting verbally, and as the kids got older it was "get into the bedroom all of you, lock the door and do not come out until I come get you all." Truth be told, my kids suffered more than I did, worrying whether I would end up dead, disfigured, or missing. They all saw, heard, and felt more than what I had seen as a child.

I was drinking again, out of therapy. I would drink when I felt lonely or vulnerable. I never enjoyed it anymore as it seemed like another drama, another fight, babysitting drunk people, passing men along to my friends as I was uninterested. As my kids grew, they bounced back and forth every six months from foster house to my house. Always a story to move back to another house, the older ones learned there were no consequences for their actions if they kept moving back and forth. The last time they left my house, I signed my parental rights over to Chief and council as they are the caregiver to children in care for our band. I had a job opportunity but had to move into a seasonal country setting.

I packed up our house and we moved in with my best friend to begin our new lives. Unfortunately, we left with the clothes on our backs and what money I had left in my bank. We started over, slowly. I felt lost with no one to ask for help or guidance, so I thought. I never reached out to anyone who could help. My drinking buddies would never say go see a therapist or an alcohol drug counselor. I was losing my spirituality again just having a pity party by myself in front of my youngest ones. I knew I had to make changes and as fast as possible for I had pondered giving up my youngest ones into care until they aged out.

The medicine man helper was the First Nation worker in the kid's school. We connected and talked. I volunteered helping her where I could, seeing both therapist and alcohol and drug counselor, working on myself hard.

I wanted to find out why I was the way I was and what did I have to do to be a better me. I was still drinking to ward off my loneliness; I was doing therapy in person and over the phone. The kids were in therapy for a while off and on until they said they didn't want to be any longer. I thought it would be good for them to start healing young and not wait until adulthood.

I reconnected with one of my sister's teen years friend who tried asking me out when he was fourteen and I was twenty-two. I was with my abuser then and scared for his life. It was like almost no time had passed. Our friendship was wonderful, but I was guarded. We've been together twelve and a half years and married for five. The beginning was rocky with alcohol fueled fights, not wanting to go down a hole, I pulled myself out. I told him he also needed help with his addictions if we were going to be together.

My husband got an alcohol drug counselor and started seeing a counselor, stopped drinking (a month before I did, scared he wouldn't follow through) and went to A.A. for ninety meetings in ninety days. I continued talking with a therapist. We have both changed from A.A. to a First Nation group called White Bison Wellbriety movement. Through online meetings now as my husband has 2904 days sober and five years being off cocaine.

I am proud to say this is the longest I have been sober, 2876 days. Believe me, we had our differences, but I felt most understood by him, no urge to drink. This year our eight-year-old Chihuahua passed suddenly. I wanted to drink the pain away.

Recently, I had to make the difficult choice to call the band child welfare on my daughter for making poor life choices. I called child welfare to protect my granddaughter. At eighteen months, she has brought life back into our grown-up house. I have a relationship with my middle child, clean, honest, and open. As you read this, I know this was not a fairytale, just a warrior's story.

Tonya K. Austin

Phone: (248) 842-8671

Email: coachtonya2020@gmail.com.

Facebook: www.facebook.com/tonyatheuthoraustin

You Tube: The Trauma Recovery Room

While many choose to hide behind their shame, guilt, and error, she chooses not to wear a mask at all, making herself vulnerable, yet unapologetically authentic, to those around her. From growing up in a toxic environment, to identity crisis's, to her own two broken marriages, and loneliness, Tonya K. Austin has made it her mission to help heal those who have been emotionally broken and heartbroken---including herself.

Having graduated Cum Laude, Tonya K holds two degrees, one being Behavioral Science with a specialty in repairing emotional damage caused by mental illness. Using her Psychology background, she puts her specialty to the test through her online courses, eBooks, books, social media content, and the best of all, through word of mouth.

Her debut book, Mending a Broken Heart, was released in 2016, and she is currently working to rebrand her entire business to fit her newest version of herself. Her sophomore book is due to be released in the middle months of the next year. She will also offer her exclusive 12-week "Do or Die" Spiritual Transformational coaching program very soon.

"When the God in Me Made Me Rise"

It took 44 years for the God *within* me to show up and show
out! It showed up so hard that it made me rise from the filthy, muddy
life I had subconsciously gotten myself into. My rise was from the
shackles of defeat, constant abuse, poverty, fear, and self-hate. As you
can imagine through your own experiences in some of these areas,
these are not easy feats to overcome.

I was worth it, and it felt good finally telling myself that for the
first time in my life. For the 30 plus years prior to that moment of
clarity in my life, I was left walking around with all those emotional
scars from my childhood that would uncontrollably haunt me, until
they were healed.

Nonetheless, I was excited to see what would come of my
choice to finally put the woman I saw in the mirror every day, with
disgust and anger having made all those wrong past choices, first and
seeing who she would become from that moment on. You see, I was a
very co-dependent individual that wanted attention, love, and
validation so badly because my soul was really starving for it. I would
settle for way less than I really knew I deserved. Because of the
negative thoughts I carried around within my head about myself, living
a full life of abundance was impossible for me.

Every day, that negativity would pop its ugly head up and
remind me of the false self I was conditioned to believe growing up.

I would yearn to have that same "confidence" I saw in others because mine was a mask I was wearing to cover up my insecurities--- or false beliefs about who I really was. Maybe, I was not the only one wearing a mask covering up pain though. I say that because sometimes I would smell that same insecure "perfume" I wore on others, but they wore it so well that I would question whether I was the only one that felt this way. Yeah, it was always my "own" fragrance that I would smell (at least I was convinced of yet, this other lie). I did not know, or it was hard to tell anyway. All I knew is that my life needed to get better and the time to do it was now.

The two most dangerous places I needed to start in this journey were my darkest ones. They came in the form of putting others before me and accepting abuse in my everyday home life. The most challenging thing for me to do was to give myself permission to be happy and enjoy being me. I never had a chance to do either of them because of the horrible things that took place in my childhood between the ages of about 4-17 years old, which led to other things later happening in my adulthood.

I will start with the issue of being molested as a child, since it was the very beginning of my emotional woes being handed right over to me. I was only between the ages of about 4 and 12 years old when it happened. It was done by a close family friend and I was not the only one he had done this to. From this experience, I was left to figure out "why this happened to me," all by myself. I knew my mother well enough to know that she would have murdered that man if she had known what he was doing.

Not that she would have helped me get through it though. So, I called myself "protecting" her, by neglecting myself. It was the very beginning of my trait developing as "Ms. Co-dependent".

That lonely and traumatic situation taught me to put others before myself and ignore my inner call for help---always worry about me later. I did not have an emotional escape for help or a loving and caring support system to escape to while growing up. I was, however, innately given the gift of helping others through my own pain which is what I do now as a Trauma Recovery Life Coach. My gift has just been distortedly seen on how to do it the right way, without hurting myself in the process. That painful moment of my life taught me to think negatively about myself, to keep quiet about what is going on within or with me, and to put others' needs before my own. A hard pill to swallow, especially at such a young age, but one I often choked on as it went down. I do not think that I was ever threatened by my molester to "keep it secret or else," but it must have been something that made me feel that way---probably my thoughts about my mother--- that kept me from getting myself the help I needed.

Because I learned to silence my mouth and protect my abuser, I would repeat those traits later in my life. I did this by frequently involving myself with abusive partners and covering things up for their protection instead of reaching out for the help and protection I always needed for myself. It was the curse of my negative experiences that would always torture my mind and soul.

Subconsciously, I was designed to "fix" the broken and emotionally hurt little girl inside of me. Those negative thoughts turned toxic and abusive relationships would one day bring me to my knees praying for the release of them---to set me free.

I never knew that hurt little girl was still inside of me wanting and desperately needing help. I never knew that the men in my past and present life would or did reflect every traumatic thing I ever faced in my childhood, with the one after the last being worse than the one before. I never knew that healing was even an option for me and that if I did not take the time to heal from the pain caused in my childhood that the "love" I was getting would only get worse---until I did. I never knew that the man I "loved" the most would end up being the one that brought me the most pain. He hurt me through his tumultuous narcissistic ways of showing his "love" for me.

I did, however, know that the way I was feeling inside was not right and that something needed to be done---that internal God kept silently calling me. I began to know that by not healing from my old wounds, it allowed the adult me to continue to stay broken and suffer from what would be the constant/uncontrollable/untamable pain of mine to continue to come. That sexual violation on my body was a massive emotional violation on my mind as well. The negative thoughts I developed about myself, would later send me down a spiraling path of promiscuity, substance abuse, shame, and multiple opportunities of bodily harm to later overcome. I was raped over four times as an adult.

For years, I would try to cover up my dirtiness and think that I was no good to a good man because of this sexually filthy experience. It gave me this false notion, along with the other incidences of destruction to my self-esteem and self-worth that I highly trusted and believed in. It would later be revealed that there were others within my family he had done this to as well, one including his own daughter who later faced the sexuality issues of what preference she would have in a mate.

For me, I needed to be fixed because clearly, I was a problem to the world, so my ego's development was very poorly done. Now the problem with this would be that I did not know how to "fix" me or where to even begin. Already, I had been left unprotected and unable to cry out for help and this was before the age of only 10-years old. Unfortunately, this was only the beginning of my destiny unknowingly being revealed to me. Each trial would only prepare me for the next, which would ultimately lead me to finding out what my purpose in life was. Each time, I would get through it, and oftentimes all on my own.

This traumatic sexual experience left me feeling like I was all alone in the world and that it was just me against the world. There was one time, however, when I saw a ray of hope in telling somebody about what I was going through. It was quickly lost when I told my friend about it and she laughed it off and said nonchalantly, "Stop lying, that didn't happen." Well, from that moment forward until the age of 21-years old, that is exactly what I did. That would have been the very moment when I learned to keep my truth quiet because nobody wanted to hear it or would believe it anyway.

At that moment, I began to start to subconsciously trust and believe in yet another lie about myself or my needs---that I or what I was going through was always a lie and that it needed not be told to others as truth. I had to come up with this lie to make things make sense in my head. It would be a lie that I would strongly accept as fact and it would be one that I would have to fight the hardest to overcome as well.

You can see what led up to my marrying an abusive man, can't you? I know I can just by writing this. So, let me continue so you can get the full effect and learn how to get through your own intricate details of healing your broken and wounded heart and making more informed relationship choices in your life. As I am writing this, it hurts my spirit to know that I had to endure all of this at such a young impressionable age, even if it was my own overall destiny unveiling. I mean, I have a baby girl that is 11-years old and to think if she were experiencing any of this AND by herself is terrifying to even think of.

Whew! That is just too much to conceive and it brings tears to my eyes now, as it did then, when I went through it. Not to mention that she would be *thinking* there was nobody around who cared enough to "see" her pain. To "see" that she needed help---because they have "proven it to her time and time again" they did not care by ignoring her. Having to keep her feelings about all the hurt she experienced trapped inside and feeling lonely and confused about what was going on and why it had to be her, it all just kills me.

That is also a hard pill to swallow, but it must be done if the world is to no longer see this thing, that destroys so many lives, called childhood trauma caused by abuse. Abuse is abuse, and whatever form it comes in is wrong. I want to see justice for all those who have had to endure the pain that comes along with it. Many abusers find themselves knowing exactly who to target and that is why they are so successful at it.

If the "victim" learns how to empower themselves (like reading this book) to prevent future occurrences from happening, and healing from it, then the issue would be on its way to disappearing. This starts after making the choice to do something about it and heal. Then after you heal, your job is to tell your story to help others do the same thing you did, like I am doing with you now. There is power in our voices and there is purpose in our pain. These two matched up to fight the woes of the enemy gives those like us who want to end it, a powerful push in the right direction.

Now, back to my story about my challenged life and how I changed it all to fit more of what I was created to do. My next reason for choosing wrongly in my life, came from an incident when I was about 11-years old. This is when I developed my internal issues about my body. I was innocently shamed for how I was divinely structured which is petite and thin with very little curves, by a boy I liked and had called my boyfriend since kindergarten. From this incident, I grew to the point of not feeling comfortable about the way I looked or how my body was shaped. I mostly felt this way in front of other women with "better bodies" than mine.

When I graduated from elementary to middle school, my boyfriend (do not judge me, but clearly I was in search of the male father or protector in my life if I was this young having a "boyfriend") I was going with, dumped me for another girl that (as he explained), was "prettier" than me and "had a better body" than mine.

Now, at 11-years old, this is drastic and detrimental to a girl's self-esteem and self-image. I started to see myself as useless, unlovable, and undesirable to *black* men, the ones that looked like me. This is a big factor of concern in the black community for women. It is a stereotype that all black women have big butts (what black men love the most), and for someone to dump me because I did not have one, made this an even bigger reality for me, personally.

Mixed with the feelings of not feeling connected, not feeling loved already from the sexual abuse, and not feeling as if I belonged anywhere (that stemmed from the parental abandonment or the constant being left alone by them), this was not a safe energy space for me to be in emotionally. I was left devastated to pick up all the broken pieces of my heart alone (again) and all those painful emotions were unable to get resolved properly because of it. I was a lost child in an emotional abyss that seemed to never end. It was tortuous most of those lonely days. Some days I even felt I no longer wanted to live, but the Creator within me always knew that God had my soul right in His hands to comfort and keep me safe, until I was old enough to do it on my own. Which was now.

Since, my mother never had time for a child, I knew going to her would have been another opportunity for her to reject me and give some more attention to her favorite daughter out of the three that lived in our home. I will talk about this traumatic experience a little later. That was a self-made observation of a 11-year old child, by the way, who felt abandoned and all alone.

My father would not know what to tell me and would only say those four dreadful words, "go tell your mother" which was always a dead-end resolution, not worth wasting my emotional time on (as I just described for you). I have very few memories of my mother from my childhood and of those I do, they are not all that good because of the way she raised us. My mother was a very stern person. Today in psychology or even society, she would be referred to as an abusive parent, going off her harsh methods of discipline during child rearing. Although she had many great motherly qualities like cleaning and making sure the children had their needs met, even if it meant having somebody else meet them for her, she had some bad ones too that placed deep dark holes in my soul.

Her system of beliefs about people in general was one of them. It was always negative, and it played a serious part on how she raised all her 11 (she had 13, but two passed away in infancy) "babies." She and my father both were older in age when I was born. She was 40 and he was 49 years old, and that was an issue in its natural right on its own.

They had grown tired of raising children by the time I came, just not tired of having them. I was the last of her bunch (not my father's though). For me, that meant I would get the most worn out, battered, abused, and fed up parts of them both as my parents.

Now, let us move on to my father and the emotional damage he caused me at the age of 12-years old, which by that time, I was already drowning in an emotional swimming pool of unresolved and confusing feelings. Little did he know that the day he would get so angry with me for making a simple, childish (because I was a child) mistake and react towards his "baby girl" in the most passive aggressively displayed way by viciously yelling out, "You are the dumbest child in the world!"---he would completely destroy all that I had possibly had left emotionally within me. His words were devastating to my heart, my ego, and my mind. My soul was brought to complete and utter humiliation and disappointment. These were the most confusing feelings of all because they came from the one person in the world (I thought) would always protect me from hurt and pain; my daddy.

For the next 30 years, I would try to make every attempt to prove him wrong about me. His words would take me down a spiraled path of mental confusion, and ultimately destruction. My journey of "proof" included obtaining two hard earned college degrees and two hard earned trade certificates (both which cost me over $100,000 of debt, yet to be paid off). While these accomplishments denied his explanation of what I was, others confirmed them.

Those confirmations came in the form of two failed marriages and multiple failed businesses that left me wondering what I was born to do and if I was good enough to do it.

So, after hearing all this so far, now I can introduce you to the effects of childhood emotional abuse. After all that I had endured and moving out at only 17-years old, I had entered that big scary world my sister told me about, but with subconscious fears to guide me along the way---an emotional disaster waiting to happen. I was in my first "real" relationship and had moved into a small first timer apartment with him. He would be the very first of my daunting relationships with abusers. I would go toe-to-toe with what the world had to offer me with this 2 ½ yearlong toxic union. My sister was right---the world was big and bad. I went into my new relationship hoping for a healthier relationship with somebody who would "love" me unconditionally. WRONG ANSWER!!!

My intention was to find a healthy love, but our relationship was far from any of that; it was toxic. From that experience, I learned how not to trust men because they were liars and cheaters who abuse you. My heart (I felt) was too kind for him to be trusted holding it in his hands. He betrayed that trust multiple times with women that were literally standing right in my face. Women that called themselves my "friend," but I knew better.

That was also when my search for external approval and acceptance from my peers would begin as well. I was not able to get it from my family (where it should have stemmed from originally), so they would be the next best thing (so I thought in my unhealed mind anyway). I never got a clue that the love I was looking for was right in my own heart. I found ways to get their approval, but nothing would stay permanently, and I would eventually remove them from my life. That relationship with him also ended, along with those "friends" of mine.

He was abusive. We had one physical altercation where he ended up sleeping with a gun in his hand with the finger on the trigger, while other incidences were verbal or emotional abuse. He was a frequent cheater, and that had all become too much for me to bear. Little did I know what was to come next. That period of my life taught me to show face and act like pain meant nothing to me although it really meant everything. It is where my "tough" image started. It is where I learned "acting extremely tough" helps you to cover up your inside pain so nobody could see it or use it against you. I felt hopeless, and it saddens me now that I thought that this bad behaving man was a good man for me.

My thoughts truly did reflect who I was with. He was not at all a good man to me and leaving him and going straight to what would be my first husband, without healing my wounds at all was next. Now, this relationship would be toxic coupling number two. We did end up getting married after I gave him an ultimatum to put a ring on it or get the hell out of my life AFTER two kids and almost 5 years had passed by. I was pregnant with baby number three and at this point he was cheating and left me for an 18-year girl (that was "prettier" than me, had a better body and was lighter skinned than I was). I had not even connected the spiritual dots yet and would not until almost 20 years later after brutally leaving what I would call husband number two.

My first husband was very immature, but so was I. Cheating was the best solution to all our problems. Afterall, we both had seen it from our father's growing up and it seemed to take those insecure and unloved feelings away (at least at the time it happened), and it was much easier than facing those deeply hidden feelings we were running from. The darker the pit we were put in and continued to choose to keep ourselves in, by denying or running from it, the deeper the wound that its darkness was covering up.

My first marriage, although it lasted 14 years, was filled with many painful hardships caused by both of us--- due to our childhood pain. Thank God a separation from my second husband allowed us to befriend each other again, resolving all the issues we had with each other from our past together.

We cried, hugged, and laughed with one another, drank and chilled like the old days. It put a huge smile on both our faces and hearts. When he died, I was at peace with him, and having found that peace made my grief over losing him less painful. Thank God for that blessing. It was one joy my soul sincerely needed. He loved me (at the end of the day nothing else really mattered) and I loved him, that is for sure. May he rest in peace, knowing that his oldest daughter and our baby girls (aged 17-24) loved him just as much, as well. What we had was just an immature love that had no chance in hell of surviving. Many times, with us being best friends, I wished we only stayed friends, but I would not have my first four baby girls, if we had. In our pain there is always a pleasure or four that we get to enjoy as well.

Being freed from my first marriage, I still had not realized that my heart was bleeding and needed some serious spiritual surgery and fast. The next man, I thought would do the trick for me, but of course, you know how the story goes. He was a narcissist, yet I did not know it. I would not find that out until years after we separated what that was and that he was one. That was the reason he came into my life. He was allowed to enter to teach me how to love myself and put me first. My first two men were narcissists as well, only on the lighter side. It is amazing that when I looked back at my choices in men, they all were sent to teach me the same thing, just all on different levels. It went from mild to severely bad, and that is when I finally figured out my truth.

This next guy, I can say the blessing with him, was our daughter. That would be my 11-year old I spoke of earlier.

Him and I had a rocky union that was filled with lies, deceit, infidelity, and some abuse (just like with my first husband--- he never hit me, but name calling and other passive aggressive behaviors played a major role in our divorce). My 11-year old's dad was a pure ladies man. A true reflection of my father and deep down I hated him for it and choosing my "ugly" self to torture with other "bad ass" women with "bad ass bodies" right in my face, because you know I did not deserve any better and I was not worthy of getting it either.

This man was not it either, my 11-year old's dad, and time for us to call it quits had come. It did take me a few years of being afraid and stuck in my false tales about myself that I continued to entertain his shenanigans, including marrying another woman while we were "working things out" between us. His behaviors had gotten too ill-willed for me and I grew tired of his game playing. We stayed together for about a year and half, in total, but my beautiful blessing (my baby girl) is here to stay. I really loved him, and I think he started off loving me too, but it grew cold too fast to have been real.

My internal body had gotten too impatient with my lack of ability to get "the message", but always knew eventually, that I would. All my faculties were growing frantic when I learned what was being taught to me. By this time, it had been over 20 years since my traumas had occurred and I had many opportunities to heal, but like most, I passed them by, regrettably so---but content with not having done so, at the same time.

The guy I was "madly" in love with had finally left my life. That one hurt because he was a handsome one and he did look good on my arm. The best part is that he taught me that looks meant nothing at all in the real spiritual world. It was about how a person treated you that mattered most. The next two guys were more on the higher range of narcissism, yet I still had not discovered what that was. With one, I was granted a beautiful blessing.

One that I had always asked God for---a son---and he used his dad to be the producer of that gift. I hope he only gets his dad's good traits though like being silly, hard-working (but not for his material desires for having it) and not afraid to explore his life.

The other guy was a narcissist on a higher spectrum and would start to be the trigger that something was wrong within me that needed my attention asap. It would only take me 9 months with him to figure it out, yet it still had not come completely to me yet. So, that only meant more learning had to be done. I had moved on again without healing my wounded heart as a reflection of that.

That ultimately takes me to the granddaddy of narcs and where I finally learned my lesson. He was terrible to me, yet it took me 2 ½ years to say to hell with all this. We had not one entire day of peace during our entire relationship. He was filled with childhood wounds that he was not even ready to acknowledge he had yet, until our marriage approached its ending. Then things for him would become somewhat clear. For me, I could clearly see that he was a visibly clear mirror image of myself. All those dark places that I kept running from had stared me dead straight in the face.

What was my "tough ass" going to do? Fight, flight, or freeze were my only three options out of it. I chose to fight. For the first time in my life, I stood up for myself. I left no streaks in my mirrored reflection either. Meaning, he was not approved by God for me to be with but would be used to put an end to this emotional madness I continued to put my mind through. I touched every dirty spot I saw in that reflection and kept my window cleaner solution handy, just in case any unneeded spot showed up again.

This final learning relationship was reflecting to me fears of all kinds. I got to a point where the whole experience scared the hell out of me. I saw some extremely dark parts and it did not look pretty at all, but I kept pushing forward. I pushed through the sexual frustrations; dealing with sexual abuse and learning and understanding my sexuality/ I pushed through the infidelity. I was angry with my father for leaving us for his other women. I felt abandoned and was seeking that replacement with men. I pushed through not knowing my life's goals; I knew parts of it, but was too afraid to put them all together and live that life I knew to be right for me. And I pushed through the rage; I could never use my voice as a child or was never heard and it made me angry.

There were plenty others that I could name, but I think you pretty much get the picture I have been trying to paint for you. Yes, I know there have been bad things that have taken place in your childhood. Yes, you have made poor choices because of those bad things happening to you.

Yes, your heart is wounded. Yes, it did not have to happen to you because you did not deserve it. That is because, yes, you needed to go through them to teach and prepare you for the life's lessons pertinent to your destiny.

Yes, that is your past and it can be rewritten to reflect God's truth about you. Yes, you can heal from all that has kept you locked up in a mental prison. Yes, you can fight this battle, but know that the war is not yours to handle alone, and that Source is with you. The reason being, is that whatever it may be, it belongs to the possibility of you reaching your destiny.

The day that the God within me showed up, it showed out. I had a terribly regular, argumentative day with husband #2 the night it happened. It ended with me having my knees dropped to the floor, with my eyes filled with tears begging (once again) for the Lord to release His power unto me. I was so close to killing him, for real, like with a real knife cutting his foul-mouthed throat for talking to me nasty and foul. I would have never thought that this stage of a relationship would ever come to us. This was the man that I once loved and who I thought once was the only one out of all my men who loved me for real. Instead, I received something much greater than that, that would help me heal from my pain and more.

We must know ourselves first, before we will ever get to know God. Because it is, He who then reminds us of why we are here on this Earth. From there, we are to seek out that knowledge and truth to confirm that journey--- which will always lead us to the unveiling of who our true beings truly are.

Mine took 44 ½ years, sexual abuse, emotional abuse, verbal abuse, neglect, anger, rage, learning to forgive myself and others, and so much more to finally show up, but again, better late than never. When I heard the Lord's quiet, still voice respond in only a way I knew it was Him saying, "The strength you ask of *Me* to give to *You* (the weak version) is already within *YOU* (the strongest version). Pull it out and use it. It is time." That is when, for the first time in my entire life, I would ever not care about anybody else's feelings or needs being met. I did not care about what the response was going to be in fear of making somebody else mad (even by writing this for you to learn and grow from).

That is because this is not about fear or growth. It is not about love or pain or me. It is about telling the truth and releasing what was into the world to be found by someone else, to create what is or what could be from it. It is about telling my story, so I can see God's glory for me. It is about knowing also that this is about something even greater than me. It is about empowering myself and you to discover my own truth and you, yours.

That very divine moment of my life, I could have cared less about any of those things that once worried my Soul before that moment of receiving my transformational truth. That was the moment *when the God in me made me rise* and I left that abusive man and took that difficult, yet loving path back to that place I call home, where my heart is!

What is the God in you doing? Do you feel a rise inside of you, or maybe a stretch or yawn? No worries, your soul is working on getting your attention if it has not gotten it yet, it is your time to rise too and let go of all those things that no longer serve you. It is your time to put in the work so you can heal your own bleeding heart instead of waiting for others to do it for you.

Be the change you want to see in your life. Let go of that anchor weight that is bringing you down.   Free yourself and your soul. Rise to the occasion of healing from all your childhood trauma and adulthood emotional pain. Learn to love the most important person in your life--- you.

Resources:

The National Domestic Violence Hotline
https://www.thehotline.org/
1-800-799-7233

Safe Haven of Tarrant County
https://www.safehaventc.org/
1-877-701-7233

Stand Up Survivor Inc.
www.standupsurvivor.com
321-430-5307

Made in the USA
Columbia, SC
09 October 2020